# REBOUND

*Staging a Spiritual Comeback*

**Belinda "BJ" Foster**

Statements made and opinions expressed in this publication are those of the author and do not necessarily reflect the views of the publisher or indicate an endorsement by the publisher.

ISBN: 978-1-948777-22-3

# DEDICATION

To my hero, my incredible dad.

The man who showed me in life

that where you start,

does not have to determine where you end.

And taught me even more in death,

that how you end,

is most important of all.

Love you, dad

I'll see you on the other side.

# ACKNOWLEDGMENTS

My sincerest thanks

- To my little family (Kai, Mason & Cole) for all your love, support, patience and understanding when mom was overwhelmed and no doubt a little cranky.
- To the Jeffersons (mom,dad, & siblings) for giving me the running start I needed for this journey
- To Octavia Alexander, my bodyguard, soul protector, my friend who encouraged me to step out in my greatness and walked with me when the road grew rocky
- To Lisa Nichols, my inspiration and great motivator.
- To Mwale and Chantel Henry for gently guiding me through this uncharted and sometimes frightening writing process
- To my Savior, for never giving up on me, pushing me beyond my comfort zone, and believing I was worth saving.

# TABLE OF CONTENTS

# FOREWORD

Growing up in church, being introduced to the power of God, the power of faith very early on, I was clear that I wanted to walk through life as a disciple. What I didn't see coming was all of the challenges. All of the disruption. All of the moments of doubt, and the feelings of being stuck in quicksand and disconnected from God. The challenge of navigating through the quote-unquote religiosity.

I found myself lost at times, confused, wondering if I was going to walk it alone or wondering how to really make my way back to God. What I could have used was a book of guidelines, like this. Rebound, Staging a Spiritual Comeback is a GPS for the soul. Better than Siri. Better than Google to find your way back to your spiritual center, your spiritual core, your spiritual truth.

Whatever your religion is or if you're not attached to religion at all, it doesn't matter. This is about attaching myself to God. I needed guiding posts. Something to let me know that I was okay in my humanity. This connection wouldn't just magically come, but an active rebound was required. What my dear, brilliant, amazing friend, mentor, and Minister, BJ Foster, has put together is a work of art. And she's done so, not just writing about others who have lost their way, but from her personal experience. Giving credence to what is seldom spoken, that even the saved can lose their way. She was my way back to God. An earth angel God sent to lasso me. BJ gave me a safe place to be angry. I was angry at church. I was angry at people. I was angry because I felt so isolated. I felt like, I've done all these things right, and all these things to the best of my ability, and yet there was no outcome, nothing tangible, that I could hold on to or show for my efforts.

BJ, patiently sat with me, day after day at the coffee shop, brought the women's bible study to my home, listening to me relentlessly question. Gave me the freedom to say anything unedited. Replaying, all of the moments that I had been hurt by people who represented God's word. Hurt by many who presented an unrealistic and unattainable standard for God's work, and one by one she was able to masterfully point me to the Word of God. I quoted things I had heard that made me feel as if I was an unworthy heathen, made me feel as if I was damned and on my way directly to hell, don't pass go, don't collect $200, and all BJ would do is calmly respond, "let's find that in the Bible." And when I couldn't find those actual words in the Bible, said the way I remember them being said, she'd gently say, "well if it's not here (pointing to the bible), then that's not the case. That was one man's interpretation, one woman's interpretation." And one by one she dismantled the painful word statements of judgments that I had layered on like a sweater, like a coat, like a veil.

She took them off one by one, week after week, month after month, year after year, never giving up on me, until that broken woman no longer existed. She turned the unbelieving, wounded, hurt, bitter woman seated in front of her into a re-believer. A rebounder. She gave my faith, a jumpstart.

BJ Foster was the jumper cables to ignite my faith, the lifeline to my relationship with God being reestablished. My spirit stands as strong as it stands today because God placed BJ in my life. You were my oxygen and my water when I needed it, which gave me a chance to heal.

Thank you for showing me that God loves me and accepts me as

I am. I am forever grateful. All the millions I get to touch, you are also touching because you help me stand. When I look at the story of my life, BJ Foster is a key and critical part. Her writings are as prolific as her words. I cannot wait to read and reread. Rebound.

Lisa Nichols

# GOD INTERRUPTED

Cell phones are the single most treasured relationships in our lives today. We'll pay any price for them. We sleep with them by our sides. They are the first thing we reach for in the morning, and we'll go to any length to protect and maintain them. After all, they are our lifelines. A phone without a clear reception or constantly dropping calls would be totally unacceptable.

*If unacceptable for our cell phones, how much more for our relationship with God?*

Years ago, my dad was diagnosed with throat cancer and underwent aggressive surgery. Because he was always strong and virile, it terrified me as a young girl to see him in such a weakened state. He was the strong one. The one everyone else depended on. Most shattering was hearing the whisper of his once strong, clear voice, now barely audible. Although he spoke in full, cohesive sentences, I was only able to make out bits and pieces, leaving me guessing at the entirety of the message. In other words, speaking, but not being heard. The frustration was great I'm sure on both parts, and the distance between us slowly grew greater as I found myself avoiding the effort it took to connect.

Over time, I came to realize that this was a reflection of my relationship with God. As circumstances in my life changed—loss of a child, failed marriage, job losses—it required change on my part that would determine the closeness of our relationship. Whether I wanted it or asked for it wasn't important. Life happens to all of us. What was important was whether or not I would be willing to adjust. I knew he was speaking, and emotionally, I wanted to hear, but the effort to connect eroded the bond. I learned a hard lesson about myself during this time: I wanted God but on my terms. I wanted him to be easy, to be effortless, to be painless. Why should I have to work so hard to get to know You? I put in my little two cents worth of love on Sunday mornings and then silently criticized *His* effort and *His* ability to reach *me*. As with my dad, I maintained the niceties. We still met for family gatherings (church) and laughed about the good times (fellowship), but our personal relationship grew more and more distant. Why? I had an attitude with God. We were connected in appearance but disconnected in power. He simply became a dropped call, one, unfortunately, I grew accustomed to and accepted as part of the journey.

For many of us, we wander like the Israelites through our spiritual journey the same way, desperate for a reception that will carry us the distance. Instead, we settle for a sporadic Sunday to Sunday God connection, leaving us frustrated and dissatisfied. Everyone else around me *seems* connected. So blindly we continue, day after day, week after week, year after year…wandering, failing to realize that there's no longer a signal. Too busy or too conditioned to seek the reason the call dropped in the first place, we just continue to hit *redial* and *hope* for a better connection. I've come to call this "God Interrupted!"

*"You were running a good race. Who cut in on you to keep you from obeying the truth?" (Gal. 5:7)*

Sadly, it happens every day in the lives of God-fearing Christians, and we never see it coming.

Ever run to the grocery store to pick up one thing and come out with everything except the one item you went in for? You entered the store so sure. I had my eye on the prize. This was going to be one of those quick in-and-out runs. Minutes into entering the store I'm asking myself, "What was it I came here for?" Now if you're like me, you chalk it up to "old brain syndrome." I tell myself to walk around and it will come to me. Ten minutes later I'm at the checkout stand with a basket full of miscellaneous items, certain the forgotten item is among them, only to discover when I get home it is not. Unwilling to go back, I simply make do with what I have.

What happened? It was only one thing. The call was crystal clear. But the assault of choices (cookies, magazines) and distractions (babies crying) allows us to wander without being aware that the call has even been dropped, continuing the conversation with no connection on the other end. We find ourselves simply talking to ourselves.

If periodic dropped calls and static-filled reception works for you in your relationship with God, then I applaud you and wish you well. This book, however, is for those seeking clarity. Those tired of wandering in the religious fog. Those seeking a connection you can count on—Christians, like me, who have found themselves craving God in a world surrounded by religious static. I'm asking you to join me on a journey to spiritual renewal. A renewal that begins with you! You, staging a spiritual comeback and reclaiming your rightful place with the Father, forgetting all the personal hype you've sold yourself and standing bare before the mirror of God. Are you willing to strip naked spiritually? The mere mention of stripping naked is terrifying, I know. We live in a society of cover-up, and we've mastered the art of camouflage. We've convinced ourselves that we look like our celebrity of choice, and with the proper makeup application, soft lighting, and expensive outfit, WE DO!

This journey, however, is about starting over, removing the façade, quieting the noise of religion, sitting at the feet of Jesus, and reconnecting.

*"Let us throw off everything that hinders and the sin that so easily entangles." (Heb. 12:1)*

After every chapter, you will find a Naked Reflections study. This is your opportunity to strip bare. You've heard the saying "dance like nobody's watching." I'm asking you to get real like nobody's watching.

If we're really going to commune with God, we have to start by being honest and admitting that we, God's people, are churches full of disconnected Christians.

My prayer is that you will dare to go deep.

Let me be the one to start.

Let me lead the way by saying…

Hello God, this is me. It's finally time I met you.

BJ

# 1

## HELLO GOD, ARE YOU THERE?

I'm on the phone chatting with a friend who, let's just say, can be a bit long-winded. Now as a disclaimer it was the end of a very long day. We were having a great back-and-forth conversation when we reached a point when I heard sound, but words were no longer coherent. To the melodic sound of her voice, I drift into the "uh-um" stage. Then, slowly, the lovely sound of snoring made its way across the airwaves.

I had fallen asleep! I say it was brief, but to hear her tell it, quite a few minutes ticked away before she realized I was on the line but no longer listening. Softly but emphatically, I began to hear my name being called over and over again. It took a while but my friend had finally realized that I was no longer with her. We died laughing when she finally jolted me back into reality. So many years have passed since that conversation, but if we were to run into each other today, the conversation would no doubt turn to the night I fell asleep on her, and laughter would arise as if it were yesterday. A funny moment between two friends—one, no doubt, that will be used to embarrass me forever.

To be honest, however, there were times when I felt that God had fallen asleep on me. I'm talking, but He's not listening. Maybe an occasional "uh-uh" to let me know He's still there, but no real connection. It's in these times I come face to face with the real me. Not the Christian of twenty-plus years, not the good sister soldier me, but the angry, manipulating, tantrum-throwing me. Those times when we forget who's God. Or least I do and start expecting, and demanding answers, obedience, and even submission from the Creator. This is ugly to say aloud, I know, but if we're going to reconnect with God, we have to come to Him in truth. The truth is, I'm a mess. My heart and my mind can go to ugly places, especially when I'm disconnected. It's where I'm most vulnerable because it's where I'm most exposed. When I'm exposed, I'm like a cat cornered in a dark alley. I attack because it's ultimately you or me.

We were innocent kids playing in the streets on a hot summer day when an older white man pulled up to ask for directions. I recall thinking how strange it was that he had managed to get lost here in this neighborhood. You see, a white person in the hood in the late '60s was an anomaly. The other kids started shouting out directions as best kids can from the street curb as they continued to run and play.

I was the quiet one. The loner. Startled when he singled me out and called me over, I was hesitant. Then he extended his hand out the car window with the one lure that speaks to a kid growing up poor: money. The area he was looking for had a shortcut that all the kids knew about, but few grown-ups traveled to.

"Can you show me the shortcut route?" he asked. "I'll pay you."

Heart pounding, I began to mumble directions for him to travel.

"I can't hear you from over there," he said. "Come here. I don't bite."

My gut said no as I approached the car. After all, there were two other kids out playing as well, and you never said no to a grown-up, especially a white one. As I got closer, the silver coins dangling outside the car window in his hand were moved inside. On the passenger seat there was more loose change than I had ever seen, glistening in the sunlight.

As he watched me eyeing the coins, he said, "Take it. You can have as much as you'd like." But that reach, as we all know, was deadly. He wasn't an innocent man looking for directions. He exposed himself then grabbed my arm.

A cat cornered in a dark alley, I fought for dear life. I attacked because it was him or me. Managing to free myself, I ran home as fast as I could. Traumatized, I said nothing but remembered everything. A week later when a girl in the neighborhood came up missing and was eventually found raped and murdered along the "shortcut," I silently blamed myself. As though a sock had been placed down my throat, there were no words I could utter, but my thoughts ran rampant. Was he the same man? That could have been me. That should have been me. God, why was I still alive and she was not? My little person's brain couldn't understand the evil of people and certainly couldn't grasp the silence of God.

Hello God, are you there?

Fast forward decades later, and I started to see the huge crack in my faith that possibly began the day that little girl got away. When I couldn't understand the move of God, I questioned the goodness of God.

One example of that was the loss of my child. To suffer a miscarriage, unfortunately, is nothing unique. But for every woman who has experienced this loss, it haunts you as you question your every move. What did I do wrong? Why didn't I do more? What could I have done differently? Did I really want this child? The list goes on and on.

Angry, I internally berated myself for everything I had ever done in life. Every late-night party attended, every lie ever told, every impure thought to cross my mind. There had to be blame placed somewhere.

Why not on me? After eventually running out of things to beat myself up over, I got angry at God and my disconnect began. Satan had led me to that place where we question the goodness of God. But I'm a Christian! Being angry with God was unacceptable! Every "good" Christian knows that! So never expressing it outwardly, the anger took up residence inside and burned fiercely. Who is this God that claims to love yet deserts you in your time of need? This is what I had prayed for. I had always desired to be a mom, and You'd promised to give me the desires of my heart. Instead, had You fallen asleep on me? Obviously, You didn't really care. I began to tumble down that slippery slope, asking:

Hello God, are you there?

I don't believe I'm the only Christian to question the goodness of God. Or the only one to wrestle with understanding God's choices in my life. Where do you go when God remains silent? What burns inside of you when you don't understand?

Oh, if I knew then what I know now. But as the saying goes, "To be old and wise you must first be young and stupid." When God appears to be silent, it is then that He is most at work.

Sitting at the computer doing the work of God three months into my well-planned, well-cared-for pregnancy, I began to spot. No, no, no. This is not supposed to be happening, God. This is not what we agreed upon. I tapped my husband that there was a problem with the baby. The ride to the emergency room seemed eternal. My husband was speaking, trying to comfort and calm my nerves, but I heard nothing. I was having an internal conversation with God, faith and anger meeting again in a fierce battle.

It seemed the room was packed with people as I waited and waited to be seen. After a brief introduction and explanation of what was going on with me, the doctor disappeared. Left again with nothing but my thoughts, I prayed, I begged, I pleaded, and I bargained with God to spare my baby. Many trips to the bathroom as the bleeding grew heavier told the story, but I refused the answer. Continuing the wait, the part of me that knew the truth wrestled with the part of me fighting to hold on to the lie. Then, outside the thin curtain, I heard the doctor's voice. Finally, I thought, he's coming to tell me to rest and that everything was okay. Instead, I overheard him speaking to the nurse.

"We need this room," he said. "Get her cleaned up. It's just a miscarriage."

And he never came back into the room.

Devastated, tears flowed from a well that seemed never-ending.

Then God walked in.

You see, I believe that in our darkest hour God shows Himself just to prove that He is there and has always been there. Answering with a resounding, "Yes, I am here!"

Despondent and desperate for a morsel of faith to hold on to I will never forget the angel God sent to me at that moment. In walked this little black nurse, Chocolate like me. Round like me. With a baked-in, warm southern accent, like me. She looked at me with the most beholding eyes, patted my leg, and said, "Baby, God must love you an awful lot" Those words floored me as though God was personally sending me a message. "At this stage, those cells are splitting so rapidly, and something didn't quite connect the way He wanted, and He's got other plans for you. Now go ahead. Get dressed. You're gonna be okay."

I had never seen her before in my life and have never seen her since, but she was the instrument used by God to comfort the disturbed. I believe the face of God changes so that we can best receive Him. On that day He showed Himself as a mother to a young girl, hurting as only a mother could understand.

Hello God, are you there? Always.

## NAKED REFLECTION

### Theme Scripture: Isaiah 61:10

> *"I will greatly rejoice in the Lord; my soul shall exult in my God, for he has clothed me with the garments of salvation; he has covered me with the robe of righteousness, as a bridegroom decks himself like a priest with a beautiful headdress, and as a bride adorns herself with her jewels."*

**Prayer:** God, if I'm honest, there have been times when I needed You most, that I felt You weren't there. I felt You were busy with others, or my problem simply wasn't important, and I was left alone to fend for myself. When I didn't understand Your silence, I quietly grew angry and resentful. I've allowed Satan to use my quiet reservations to place a wedge between us. Forgive me. Cleanse me within so that I can again stand heart to heart with the one who loves me unconditionally. Amen.

## NAKED STUDY

Are you ready to undress?

The greatest trap of Christians is self-deception. It's so easy to deceive ourselves that we are or are not what we need to be for God. There's something very unsettling about standing before God bare and allowing Him to show us what we need to see in ourselves. We either try to beat Him to the punch or close our eyes to the truth anticipating pain. The problem with that, however, is no matter which direction we lean, our viewpoint is skewed.

18 Very truly I tell you, when you were younger you dressed yourself and went where you wanted, but when you are old you will stretch out your hands, and someone else will dress you and lead You where you do not want to go. 19 Jesus said this to indicate the kind of death by which Peter would glorify God. Then he said to him, follow me! (John 21: 18-19)

We've all, in our younger years, clothed ourselves to protect ourselves. Whether it's a hard outer surface to protect against bullies at school, pride to show ourselves competent at work, or arrogance to show ourselves confident to the world, we're all heavily dressed. Then God enters our lives, and we proceed to add to what we are already wearing, rather than strip down and allow Him to redress us. This naked reflection is calling you to completely undress (thoughts, fears, attitudes— no matter how "un-Christian" they may feel) so that God can redress you.

**Q.** Think back over your life, your childhood, and all that you endured. What did you do to survive it?

_____

_____

_____

_____

_____

**Q.** Without any judgment, list what got you through. What layers of self-dress can you identify?

_____

_____

_____

_____

_____

**Q.** God is asking, "Do you trust me?" No longer needing the protection you provided yourself, are you willing to stretch out your hands and let Him dress you and lead you where you do not want to go?

_____

_____

_____

_____

_____

**Q.** Jesus said this to indicate the kind of death by which Peter would glorify God. Then He said to him, "Follow me!" In your own words, how is Jesus calling you to follow Him?

_____

_____

_____

_____

_____

_____

_____

**Q.** My miscarriage was the first clear indication that I was fighting God's will in my life. Identify a specific battle with God in your life and how He showed himself for you and not against you.

_____

_____

_____

_____

_____

_____

_____

# 2

## SPIRITUAL FADE TO BLACK

Growing up in poverty, we only had so many escapisms because we only had so much money to spread around. There was penny candy that actually cost a penny. A dirt pile on the side of the road that became our castle or fortress for the day. But now and then, we had this special treat in which the whole family, and sometimes a stray neighbor or two, piled into the car to go to the drive-in movie.

Back then, they charged by the carload. So we'd pack kid on top of kid and would worry about comfort once we got inside. The movies were my great escape! On Fridays, they showed the black movies, like *Cleopatra Jones, Claudine,* and *Shaft,* starring domestics or trashmen, but they looked good on the screen. Then on Saturdays were the white movies where the actors were always dressed in beautiful gowns with meticulous hair and makeup.

We'd hang outside the fence and watch those movies without

sound. That's when I began to dream of being in the movies. I would be the tough-as-nails mama in the black movies during the weekday and dressed up in a ballgown, gracefully fainting in the white movie on the weekend. We always laughed that in the white movies someone always fainted, but never onto the ground. It was always beautifully done onto a chaise lounge.

I often wondered did this really happen? Where I'm from, fainting was only something you'd see in the movies. It made no sense to me that a grown person would one minute be standing and then all of a sudden collapse. Usually, at least in the movies, it was out of exhaustion. Exhaustion? Are you kidding me? I've watched my mom work the 11-7 nursing shift, come home and create breakfast out of nothing, get six kids off to school, and take a nap before going to the beauty shop to do hair—all before school was out at three. To the best of my knowledge, she has never fainted! It just seemed wimpy and fake.

Until, that is, it happened to me. What the heck! Black people don't faint!

I was a young college student, a track star, needing to get to the post office before they closed. I could easily sprint over with time to spare, and so I did. Now standing in line and cooling down rapidly, I started to feel a little queasy, light-headed, a little uncomfortable. Feeling the rush of heat come over my body, I tried taking a few deliberate deep breaths, willing myself to stay standing. The room began to move in slow motion, and before I knew it, I went down like a bag of dropped potatoes. I could hear voices but couldn't make out the faces around me among the commotion.

"Give her some room."

"She needs air!"

"Does anyone have some water?"

These were the shouts of the voices. Lying pitifully there on the floor, I was the wimp from the movies, totally embarrassed, saying "I'm all right" and trying to explain sheepishly what happened.

It seems to happen in a matter of seconds, and before you know what hit you, you're out. In reality, however, in those brief moments, the body is sending signals at breathtaking speeds that go unchecked, telling you, "I'm feeling light-headed, dizzy, a little weak." But with each ignored signal, I found myself physically reeling, grasping for something tangible to hold on to and eventually collapsing.

In my life, just as with the human body, there were so many things I chose to ignore. Signs, glaring signs, all pointing in the same direction, saying, "Something's wrong," "Turn back," or "Do not enter." But that train had long left the station. The little girl loving make-believe was growing up to be an expert in disguise and role-playing. Instead of the frightened, helpless girl running from a stranger, I vowed to be the tough girl who could hold her own. The fighter from the other side of the tracks, I'd say, "I wish a man would try to lay a hand on me. I'd take him out! Are you kidding me? I was raised with a house full of brothers. I'd rock his world!" I prided myself on being a strong black woman, an honor I wore boldly. It's amazing how tough you can be in your imagination, isn't it?

Unfortunately, there was an equally terrified black woman growing up inside as well, and at some point, the two would have to reconcile. So decades later, having mastered the stony I-don't-need-help-from-anyone exterior, I found myself at odds with myself, but in truth, as it says in Obadiah 1:3, I was conflicted with God: "*The pride of your heart has deceived you, you who live in the clefts of the rocks and make your home on the heights, you who say to yourself, 'Who can bring me down to the ground?'*" I was running away from the hurts of the past, potential blows of the future, and the God who I believed had turned away.

I lived my single life in isolation, buffered from all that could harm me, and believe it or not, I liked it that way. When I went to work, others did my makeup, my hair, and dressed me in the finest clothes that flattered my body. They provided me with whatever I needed. In return, I did what I did best: I performed, received the praise and accolades, and went home, all to prepare to do it again tomorrow. Scripts were expressed to my door, and cars picked me up to carry me to my various destinations. My world, to some degree, revolved around me. And I knew it.

When a successful actor says they're just a normal person, they're lying. Oh, that's your desire, to not be changed by it all, but it happens. It's like a homeless person winning the lottery. You're not accustomed to the lifestyle now thrust upon you, so you maneuver as best you can around it. There are no lessons, no blueprints in being a "celebrity." No one pulls you aside with best practice tips for staying grounded when you're not who people think you are, but you're not who you used to be, either.

My ever-changing world had shifted around me, and I was in a tug of war of sorts with myself. With each shift, God was trying to get my attention, but I simply put on another disguise and moved on. In this case, I faked humility and pushed away, as best I could, the privilege of it all, but inside I knew that I no longer had to live the hard life I had come from. Life as I had known it had changed. It wasn't by any stretch of the imagination "stardom," but God had answered prayers and eased the struggle of day to day survival, desiring I'm sure to turn me toward Him. The funny thing about being delivered, as we see in Deut. 8:10-11, is that it's so easy to forget the deliverer. *"When you have eaten and are satisfied, praise the LORD your God for the good land he has given you. Be careful that you do not forget the LORD your God."*

Now, I rode the subway train because I wanted to, not because I had to. I lived in Harlem because it was chic, not because I had to. It's hard to explain unless you lived it, but the world of entertainment is very surreal. You love it and you hate it. You pull it close while also pushing it away. In all honesty, people had become an annoyance to me. They were something to be tolerated, simply to be used to keep the magazines interested and the photographers snapping. I feel sick to my stomach as the words appear on the page, but if I'm showing my road to healing, I have to be willing to show the extent of my sickness. People, for me, God's people, beautifully made in the image of the Father, had become dispensable.

Rom. 10: 12, "Be devoted to one another in love. Honor one another above yourselves."

I pull back the curtain of my life, not so that the world can be a voyeur into another messed up life of an entertainer—we have magazines on the stands for that—but rather so that someone can find their healing through my pain. What do you do when you find yourself in conflict with the Almighty? Trust me, it's not just an actor's problem, but a problem of teachers, dishwashers, students. It's universal. I could put it in a softer, maybe more palatable way and say I was struggling with obedience, but the harsher reality is, I thought I knew better. He was wrong and I was right. Yeah, I thought the Creator of the world had made a huge mistake by calling me to open myself up to people. After all, I didn't trust people, which is why I shut them out to begin with. In my then thirty-three years of living, I had, by Christians and non-Christians alike, been lied to, cheated on, deceived, disparaged, and vilified. Who in their right mind would deliberately open the door to that kind of heartbreak? My circumstances called for an exception, right? Then I remember Jesus and all the horrible descriptions that can be used to depict the assault on Him during His thirty-three years here on Earth, by Christians and non-Christians alike, and I am silenced.

So again I ask, what do you do when you're in conflict with the Almighty…and you know it?

Psalm 81:12, "So I gave them up to their stubborn hearts to follow their own devices."

That's a scary passage of scripture, isn't it? It is designed to move us to repentance, and I wish I could say it landed on a responsive heart, but

I continued for months living life by my rules, and on my terms thinking somehow I was punishing the God who had fallen asleep on me. Maybe I could outmaneuver or convince Him to change His mind and allow me to live my life alone, comfortably nestled in my hurt. He was calling me to submit my life to him *(Submit yourselves, then, to God; Jam. 4:7)*, but like a rookie boxer against a champ, I stood in defiance, determined to fight.

What about you, how do you fight against God? Truth of the matter is you picked up this book because you desperately need to rebound from the hits of the enemy, but also from the exhaustion of sparring with God.

*"God is not man, that he should lie, or a son of man, that he should change his mind. Has he said, and will he not do it? Or has He spoken, and will he not fulfill it?"* (Num. 23:19)

Gentle, yet persistent, He allowed my fortress of protection that I had built to start closing in on me. The silence was deafening. The noise of the television or music on the radio couldn't drown it out. Time with friends did nothing because this wasn't about my surroundings. It was internal. My faith was in crisis. God was speaking, and I had shut the door of my heart, locked it, and thrown away the key. Running from His will in my life, I was spiritually fading to black but ignoring the signs. I was growing faint, but just as the young me in the post office, I was so sure I could control what was happening, so I buckled down and pushed through. I could have won an Oscar in the role of "pushing through." Most things I accomplished were from sheer will and determination because when my fear rises, the fighter emerges. Unfortunately, I was fighting against God, the GOAT (greatest of all time), and chances are, in some area of your life, so are you.

Your fight may look different. I pushed people away. Maybe you busy yourself with people to keep from hearing what God is saying. Possibly hide behind tears and emotion that's always a good one. Surely God will go easy on me if He sees how delicate I am, right? Wrong. When

God has you on the ropes, He has you there for a reason and will not let up until the mission is accomplished.

I recall coming home one Friday evening, checking my voice messages, something I did every day, but today was different. Message after message went like this: "BJ, we have an interview for you Monday morning, give a call back." "BJ, you have a final callback for a new sitcom, can't wait to talk about it." "BJ, we've got a commercial booking for you, congratulations, talk soon." All wonderful things to rejoice over. But that evening, listening to those messages, God penetrated the locked door of my heart, and I broke down.

Reality washed over me. There was not one personal message. No "BJ, girl, I was just thinking about you and wanted to say hey" in the whole bunch. At that moment, it hit me like a ton of bricks, and I cried out in anguish. "God, if I were to die in this apartment tonight, no one would know or care until I didn't show up for an appointment Monday morning." I had built an impenetrable tower around myself, and unfortunately, I had locked myself in. In His compassion, He was calling me to draw near to Him (come near to God and he will come near to you: Jam. 4:8), yet in my rebellion, I answered no.

Are you pushing back against God?

Trauma makes for a strange bed partner, and it causes us to do the most unpredictable things. Satan knows it and, in his deviousness, waits for a more opportune time. But thankfully, we serve a God who steps into our messes with us.

There's a saying in domestic abuse circles: "Sometimes giving someone a second chance is like giving them an extra bullet for their gun because they missed you the first time."

Over the years God's call for me to draw closer to him went unanswered. Fast-forward several years, and I gave the enemy his extra bullet. An abuser, they say, can smell those easily manipulated, making you an easy target. I didn't want to believe that to be me. Remember, I was the strong black woman I told you about earlier. But having not dealt with my opposition to God coupled with my "I got this" exterior, the nightmare began, but on a level that I couldn't imagine. What has made this chapter so difficult to write is that even after thirty years, there is still a strong urge to remain silent, to protect the abuser. Make sure you don't say anything that's going to upset or disrupt the calm. Wow, the grip of Satan is powerful and far-reaching. It's been decades since I've stepped back into this part of my life, yet we are somehow still intertwined.

To rebound you must come face to face with what's holding you down. The gravitational pull keeping you earthbound instead of heavenly focused. Usually, it takes on the face of a person or persons that have hurt us, abandoned us or disappointed us, but in truth it's a higher struggle.

*For our struggle is not against flesh and blood, but against the rulers, against the authorities, against the powers of this dark world and against the spiritual forces of evil in the heavenly realms. (Eph. 6:12)*

Randomly house cleaning, I stumbled upon drawers chock full of empty or near-empty little brown vials. That's strange, I thought. What is this? Why would you hold on to empty bottles? Temporarily confused, I wasn't sure at first of what I was seeing, but the unmistakable white powder in the bottom announced itself. A marriage already on the rocks, add in drugs and alcohol, and an explosion was bound to happen. Like in a movie, my life slowly shifted into flashbacks. The erratic behavior, constant sniffling, running nose, over-excitement, paranoia…it was all coming into focus. For five long years, I thought I was going crazy. I mean, he's so personable, crazy talented, loved by everyone, so why are you so suspicious, BJ? Is it envy, jealousy? That happens a lot with dueling entertainment couples. What's your problem?

I had heaped blame on myself for being unreasonable. As money disappeared from the accounts, I berated the banks for their incompetence and irresponsibility, threatening to sue. A signal ignored. Anger erupting over the smallest thing, followed by bloodcurdling threats of "don't you dare say anything." A signal ignored. Finding myself thrusted against the wall, face to face with a fiery mandate: Trust somehow irrevocably broken. A signal ignored. Degrading outbursts, "I would never let you have my child," spewed in disgust as I sat stoic, the tough girl, the protector, attempting to brush it off. Signal ignored. In that surreal moment, my beautiful smiling face flashed on the TV screen selling some product I don't recall, but in stark contrast to the hellish nightmare I was literally standing in. Years of abuse culminating into one moment. It was the night I spiritually faded to black. No more fight left in me. Falling to my knees, I finally waved the white flag of surrender.

Hello God, are You there? I'm dying. Have You forgotten me? Depleted and dejected, I found myself looking out my seventh-floor bedroom window onto the barb-wired fence and concrete below, wondering if this was my only way out.

"You are not forgotten, and I am never far from you" was the voice that echoed in my head.

When Thomas adamantly proclaimed in John 20, *"Unless I see the nail marks in his hands and put my finger where the nails were, and put my hand into his side, I will not believe,"* I don't believe he was doubting Christ, but his ability to go on without Him. The trauma of witnessing the crucifixion had collided with Thomas's limited understanding. His faith was in crisis. Here I stood, like Thomas, my faith in shambles, doubting, questioning, God, where are You? But then something miraculous happens in John 20: 27. Jesus shows up. Then He said to Thomas, *"Put your finger here; see my hands. Reach out your hand and put it into my side. Stop doubting and believe."*

"What was miraculous about that, BJ?" you're probably asking. Jesus, you see, had already come and comforted the disciples the week before, but Thomas, the one, at that moment, stuck in doubt and needing Him most, wasn't there. He came through the locked door, I believe, of Thomas's waning heart and met him in his hurting place. Jesus came for

His one who had gotten lost in the haze. It was a miracle just for Thomas.

The voice in my head that night was the outstretched hand of God saying, "BJ, you are not forgotten and I am never far from you." Jesus came into my hurting place, took my hand, and led me away from what at that moment, was an alluring out and into a place of security with Him. It was a miracle just for me.

*Jam. 4: 10, Humble yourselves before the Lord, and he will lift you up.*

## NAKED REFLECTION

### Theme Scripture: John 3:18

*"Whoever believes in him is not condemned, but whoever does not believe stands condemned already because they have not believed in the name of God's one and only Son."*

**Prayer:** *Father, so many times I find myself on the brink of destruction, having forsaken Your will for my own. Help me to trust You, help me to believe You, and help me not to doubt You. Thank You for being willing to come to the edge, for a sinner like me. Amen.*

## NAKED STUDY

Pride and rebellion can take us to scary places. What is it about getting close to the edge before waving the flag of surrender that is so tantalizing? The thrill of roller-coaster rides or standing out over the Grand Canyon on a glass-bottom floor. It's rooted in our DNA. We see it in Sampson as he plays close to the edge with Delilah, with David as he entertains the thought of Bathsheba. And in our lives, as we dance with danger. It's the inner war within us fighting for lordship.

**Q.** What are you in conflict over with God in your life? What are you battling?

_____

_____

_____

_____

_____

_____

_____

**Q.** What toll has holding onto your will taken on your life?

_____

_____

_____

_____

_____

_____

**Q.** What toll has it taken on your relationship with God?

_____

_____

_____

_____

_____

_____

**Q.** What hurting place of yours has Jesus stepped into, and how did He show Himself?

_____

_____

_____

_____

_____

_____

_____

**Q.** What is God saying to you personally to call you from your ledge?

_____

_____

_____

_____

_____

_____

_____

_____

_____

# NOTES

# 3

## TREADING WATER

I was recently talking to an eight-year old kid at camp when he began sharing how he loved dirt bikes, riding his scooter, and swimming.

"So you're really good at swimming?" I asked.

"Oh yeah," he said. "I can go into the deep end of the pool and everything."

Just keeping conversation, a grown-up to a child, I smiled, shook my head, and said, "Wow! good for you. Not me, swimming is not my thing."

Amazed, he looked at me and said, "You can't swim?" Then he uttered a statement that I believe God has been trying to get me to hear all my life. "But all you have to do is stand up." His little brain had quickly accessed that if you're taller than 5 feet, then you have the upper hand.

I've come to realize just how exhausting my battle has been simply because I was fighting the water when all I had to do was stand up. Now,

27

there are so many things that he didn't understand, like the power of the undercurrent. The push and pull of the gravitational force. But what this child clearly grasped was that fear begins in my mind.

Just like me, millions of everyday Christians are living exhausted lives as we try to will ourselves through rough waters, easily trusting God in the shallow end, forced to surrender to God in the deepest, but taking the reins from God when the water starts to ebb and flow in the middle. At times it's a little choppy, but then it calms. Choppy, then calm. There's something about the middle. The yellow light. That transition of uncertainty. That place when logic says, "I should be able to handle this part." After all, I'm 5'3" and the deepest point here is only 5 feet, so if I find myself in trouble, I can get myself out. That middle ground where you don't really think you need the hand of Jesus. Of course, you'd never say it, but it's the "I'll call you when I need you" syndrome. The place where I'm waiting upon the Lord intellectually, but really handling it myself. Until I can't.

Thus says the Lord,

"Cursed is the man who trusts in mankind

And makes flesh his strength,

And whose heart turns away from the Lord."

(Jer. 17.5)

When I was called into ministry, I rejoiced and cried all at the same time. I understood the magnitude of that calling and the sacrifice it would take to step into it. Like a snake shedding its skin, the process doesn't happen as quickly and easily as it may appear to onlookers. Instead, they continuously rub up against their environment, loosening the skin they've outgrown, until they can, with ease, writhe out of it. For me, that meant I was about to start a journey of bumping up against my surroundings. Disrupting my normal. Bruising. Fighting to get out of tight spots. None of this appealed to me. Who in their right mind deliberately says yes to pain?

When given the choice, I will always choose the road of least resistance. God was about to begin that process with me, and He was calling me to willingly surrender to it. I would have to be either crazy or madly in love, and at this point, honestly, I wasn't so sure of the answer. That transition when treading water, working hard to keep my head above the surface, no longer sufficed. It was now time for me to lie back, close my eyes, and let this "invisible force," this God, take control, trusting He wouldn't let me drown. It was time to float. Something I had no idea how to do.

How are you at trusting God in transition?

I was at the peak of my career when I knew that God had something different planned for me. I was nicely comfortable in my Harlem condo being picked up by the studio car every day to take me in for my early morning calls. The lights of the Broadway stage is where I spent most nights, while the dressing room of a studio consumed my days. Weekends, on the other hand, were devoted to preaching, teaching, and sharing the word. I was pleased with my juggling act, and God must have found favor with me because the blessings kept coming. Every acting role, commercial, or voiceover booked was confirmation that all was well between the big man upstairs and me. Maybe this floating thing isn't going to be so bad after all.

My plan not God's.

Isn't it funny how pleased we can get when God does something that we agree with? Oh, but that was about to change. He was about to show up in ways that didn't meet with my approval. Didn't feel so "right" to me. You see, I had this whole transition thing planned out. First, I went to the extreme. He was going to rip everything from me. I would be called to give up everything, and like Lot, walk away from this sinful world of entertainment and never look back on it again. I had counted the cost on that scenario, swallowed deep, and prepared myself for the leap.

My plan not God's.

It was going to be painful, but I had readied myself and was saying, "Here I am, send me." But He didn't seem to be moving in that direction. The flood gates, on the contrary, seemed to be opening wider. In my great wisdom, I shifted again into the "I know what He's doing" seat. He needs me in the industry to help guide others to Him, to show them their wayward lives were opposing the Savior. Prepared to carry the torch, I wore the banner proudly that David wore in Isaiah 22:22. *"I will place on his shoulder the key to the house of David; what he opens no one can shut, and what he shuts no one can open."*

Wrong! Oh, the arrogance. He didn't make that turn, either. Jesus didn't need me as a junior savior of the entertainment world. He wasn't after "them" at all. He was after me. And for that, I had no reference. No plan. What were you up to? Like an amateur card player up against a master, I was trying to figure out God's hand and failing miserably.

Sometimes the longer we've been Christians the less surrendered we are. Instead, we become experts in trying to predict God's next move in our lives. Our plan not His.

So, He had me wait. Again, that scary place where your mind runs rampant. Along the way, I did bit parts in movies and backup vocals behind various recording artists. He allowed me to taste and see that it was good. You see, contrary to popular belief, the arts, in and of itself, isn't innately evil, any more than any other industry. Now sitting in my sweet spot, I began to bump up against my surroundings, but not at all in the way I expected. I predicted growing weary of the industry and maybe repulsed desiring more than anything for God to take me out, but it didn't happen that way. Rather, I met and fell in love with some wonderful people. People not unlike myself, gifted and in turn, using that gift to give back.

Goodness, however, was encircled by the bitter taste of this world. In the '80s, I watched in disbelief as cast members and friends became mere skeletons and dropped like flies from a new disease called AIDS.

Watching strong and vibrant men one week become emaciated and untouchable the next, broke my spirit.

I can still see my dear friend's face, unable to speak, but his eyes saying, "Will you touch me? I don't want to die alone." He had been disowned by family and abandoned by friends, and now I was being called by God to stand in an unfamiliar, undesirable, unchartered gap. Frantically treading water, I pushed back against the tide.

What do you do when God throws you into something you do not want to do? Love someone who has said terrible things about you? Forgive someone who has hurt you deeply? Help someone who has time after time turned a blind eye to your needs? Like the snake rubbing up against our habitat we protest, I protested. "God, I'm scared. This water is too deep, the cost too great. I don't want to do this!"

He said, "Do it afraid."

So, I stood holding the hands of many who no one would touch, much like Covid today, holding my breath as I awaited my own test results of a disease whose contraction methods we were still unsure of. He was purposely pushing me into tight spots, forcing me to twist and writhe to shed my skin. Preparing me to love the unlovable, touch the untouchable, and challenging my willingness to lay my life on the line. Why? God knew I had a problem loving people. He had to uproot the seed of disdain in my heart in order for me to be useful to Him. I was undergoing spiritual open-heart surgery. Masterfully designed so that I could see and acknowledge what was deep within me, selfishness camouflaging itself as self-preservation. A reluctance showing itself as caution. An indifference masking itself as reservation. To be an instrument of change for others, I had to first become changed. To do that I had to rebound from the blows of life that I had quietly tucked away.

What are you running away from? Hiding from God that He wants to do surgery on. There is no rebound without first facing truth.

I saw my desires take precedent over God's will time after time as I questioned every step, every move. This can't possibly be what you want for me. I think you're making a mistake here. I entertain people. That's what you gifted me for, right? In other words, send someone else, not me. But as a doctor to his patient He kept speaking, BJ, I am God you are not.

Once I stood in a friend's hospital room, rubbing his feet, awaiting the inevitable. Nurses kept coming to the door and peering into the small window smiling, offering up what I thought was comfort and support to a grief-stricken family. The dichotomy of the heavy sadness inside and the near giddiness outside the door was striking. Afraid to enter the "AIDS" room, they waited until I exited and gleefully diverged upon me, asking for an autograph and what it was like to be on TV. It broke me, as life and death, fantasy and reality again collided—with me stuck in the middle. God what are trying to do? It hurts too much this way. Again, my plan not God's plan.

All right, God, I get it. You can stop now. I'm throwing up the white flag. See, I surrender. If only we could tell the Father when enough is enough. There was still so much further to go. More shedding was needed. Bracing myself for more vigilant hospital visits, loss of loved ones, and pain, I held my breath and waited.

Again, He flipped the switch. Instead of hospital rooms, He took me to the board room. Just before the signing for the lead role in a network sitcom, in walked a more recognizable face and name.

"We want to do just one more read," they said.

Salaries discussed; contracts negotiated. We decided to go in another direction. Okay. I guess it wasn't meant to be. A sting, but there's always another job coming down the pike.

Along comes an audition to read for one of Hollywood's elite writers and directors. Looking over the script, there were a few questionable words, but nothing I couldn't maneuver around. After all, I'd done it before at no real cost to me. This was different though; this was Hollywood royalty. To my surprise, I was called in to meet the man himself. Hands sweating, I have a seat in his immaculate office. Then he leans over and says, "I just had to meet you." A smile came over my face. I must have wowed them with my wonderfulness. "I had to meet the young actress willing to put her career on the line and say no to me." There was something in the tone.

Smile fading, I sat there a little stunned, thinking, well, that's not exactly what I meant to do.

He went on to say, "I've been writing a long time, and no one's ever said no to saying the lines I've written on the page. I stand solidly behind the words that I've written, but I wish you well."

Everything inside me wanted to say, "Wait, I was just kidding, I'll read the script as written." Instead, I rose, shook his hand, and said "Thank you," wondering, what have I done? My heart was pounding. God, I'm not so sure about this plan. I'm willing to give it up, but do you have to lead me to the goal line then stop the play? Just shut the door already! It's less painful.

In my head I could hear God saying, 'pain avoidance is cross avoidance' and He was leading me to the cross. Are you avoiding your cross by avoiding your pain?

Role after role came fast and furious, only to slip away at the finish line, all with human praise and admiration for the woman standing on convictions. From studio heads to church leaders, I was held up as an example of sold-out commitment. It became a running joke that a person could build a resume on the number of jobs I'd turned down. Inside, however, I felt like a fraud because I was in conflict with God. Angry. I hadn't signed up to be a role model. I hadn't agreed to this move.

Feeling I'd gone as far as I could go, all skin had been shed, He placed me in the deep waters once more to see if I would revert to my default setting. We all have one, you know. That place we go to when all else fails. Mine is my own strength—sheer brute force to stay above water. We see it with the disciples in the storm in Mark 6: 47-48.

*"Later that night, the boat was in the middle of the lake, and he was alone on land. He saw the disciples straining at the oars, because the wind was against them. Shortly before dawn he went out to them walking on the lake."*

Jesus, after training and teaching, now stood back and watched to see how His disciples would respond in their present danger. Would they tread water (trusting their own ability) or float (trust what Jesus had taught)? When their waters grew rough, they did what fishermen do: they strained at the oars. Their default setting.

When the call came, I heard a tone in my agent's voice that I hadn't quite heard before. He was express messaging over a script. An offer had been made for me to play the lead role opposite one of the biggest stars of our time, and the film was being shot by a prominent director. This is an actor's dream. What you put in the hard work for. I waited with anticipation and excitement for the messenger to arrive. I curled up with a hot cup of tea and began to read and highlight the role that was about to catapult my life into the next stratosphere. With every scene, every page turned, it became increasingly more evident this one was not simply a matter of changing a few lines. The very essence of the character stood in total opposition to what I believed and who I had become. This time He didn't sweep down ahead of me, aborting the collision. But as with the disciples on the lake, He stood on the shore and watched. He watched to see. Will she return to her default setting and begin to tread water, or will she trust Me and float?

It was a restless night as I struggled to shed the last of the skin holding the new me to the old me. How would I tell my agent? He'd been through this with me before, but never on this level. What will my friends think? Will this opportunity ever come around again? All questions that I had no answer to. Ultimately, it came down to a matter of pride. Could I, a daddy's girl, sit next to my physical dad in a movie theater and be proud of what he's seeing me do on screen? If not with my earthly father, then how much more with my Father in heaven?

I laid back, closed my eyes, and for the first time began to float.

*"No one takes it from me, but I lay it down of my own accord. I have authority to lay it down and authority to take it up again. This command I received from my Father." John 10:18*

I now understood my journey of shedding. This was more than me learning to sacrifice my life, but sacrificing my life willingly. Entertainment, you see, was not my final destination, but the furnace through which I traveled to come out changed on the other side, never looking back and with no regrets.

A snake will continue to shed its skin as long as it's growing, and snakes grow all through their lives. So, it should be with us. The journey to surrender is not a one-time experience. I have to confess, after nearly thirty years of serving in churches, my post-journey in ministry has been just as tumultuous as my pre-journey getting there. Sometimes I marvel at how closely related ministry and entertainment can be. The gravitational pull to don a mask, to want to fit in at any cost, busying yourself beyond reason, never quite measuring up, and the insecurities that arise from it, the love and hate relationships surrounding you, all creating that surreal existence of being stuck in the middle of fantasy and reality.

Many times I've wanted to throw in the towel and go back to my simpler life, entertaining, taking people away from their pain for a couple of hours, where I get to turn it all off at the end of the day. Then I hear Jesus asking, in John 6:67, after many of His disciples turned back and no longer followed Him,

*"You do not want to leave too do you?"*

Just as Peter, who had come too far to turn back, I look at the distance God traveled to claim my life. The highs and the lows. Every hospital room, funeral home, and jail cell He had me enter to show His presence. Every movie role turned down and every painful word spoken from those not understanding the call and I am humbled and replied...

*Lord, to whom shall we go? You have the words of eternal life. We have come to believe and to know that you are the Holy One of God.*

## NAKED REFLECTION

### <u>Was I Worth It?</u>
### Theme Scripture: Psalm 25:3

*"Surely none who wait for You will be put to shame; but those who are faithless without cause will be disgraced."*

**Prayer:** *Father, in my arrogance and impatience, I have taken the reins from Your hands during times when You've called me to wait. I have made a mess of my life and have exhausted all energy. Father, I humbly return to You with open arms. Grant me the willingness to remain still and trust You. Amen.*

**Naked Study**

Life so often is a time of treading water, feeling like you are getting nowhere, or are simply going in circles. Jeremiah 29:11, "For I know the plans I have for you, declares the Lord, plans to prosper you and not to harm you, plans to give you hope and a future." Although God knows the plan for us, it is a time of suffering for us trying to find our way. In this Naked Reflection, the goal is to reframe our thinking on suffering as a tool God uses to guide us to our next destination. "Your sufferings are the breadcrumbs leading to your mission."

**Q.** Working diligently in one direction only to be intercepted by God and punted in another direction can seem heartless, and we often internalize the pain. Identify a direction change in your life by God and explain the love and wisdom of God in it.

_____

_____

_____

_____

_____

_____

**Q.** All of my suffering was rooted in people (hurt, distrust, disappointment, and the like) all preparing me for the mission of serving others unconditionally. Track your suffering and identify what God is showing you about your mission in life?

_____

_____

_____

_____

_____

_____

_____

_____

_____

_____

**Q.** Are you still in your "treading water" (fighting against the water and trusting in yourself) stage? If so, bravely ask yourself or someone else who knows you well, why?

_____

_____

_____

_____

_____

_____

_____

_____

_____

**Q.** Take time to look back at the distance God traveled to claim you. Write it down and share it with someone. Then ask yourself, was it worth it?

_____

_____

_____

_____

_____

_____

_____

_____

_____

_____

_____

# NOTES

# 4

## BOUND FAITH

The pastor grasped my hand as I proceeded to walk out the doors of the sanctuary. His words echoed like heels on a tile floor.

"I'm always so glad to see you. When I'm preaching, I can see that you're always right there with me. By the way, my wife and I love your work." He shook my hand and said, "Be blessed."

I smiled as I always do and said, "Thank you. Great lesson." As I turned to walk away, like a dear familiar friend, tears began to well up, flow, and comfort me.

I had walked in battered and beaten down by the emotional abuse of my marriage the night before, desperate for refuge from the prison I was living in. Life's pressures had landed heavily on me, and I couldn't lift them off. What happened? I had become so good at pushing off pressure, but today my knees were buckling, and I didn't know where else to go. The sizable checks placed in the contribution tray no longer brought relief. The stirring music and even powerful preaching weren't the answer. So yes, I sat, week after week, listening to the message and cried. I cried incessantly, not out of being moved by the spirit, but because I was adrift from the Jesus I'd once fallen in love with and didn't know how to get back.

Where is He? How do I get to Him if not through the church? I didn't want to be a star here. I needed a safe place to fall at the feet of Jesus and be free to be the mess that I was. As I descended the steps that bright Sunday morning, I knew I would never be back. Surrounded by hundreds, but completely alone, I walked to my car asking myself, "How did I end up here?" I'm just a country girl who loves God but has gotten disconnected and is trying to find her way back home. Like so many times before, again I find myself gagging on an imaginary towel stuck in my throat.

I look at the ongoing debate about the failures of our prison system that has echoed through our nation for decades. Although divided on the solution, all agree on one thing: our prison system is broken! Our correctional system is not correcting but maintaining at best and debilitating at worse. Rightfully so, we should be up in arms.

But here I stand faced with an equally seismic question, one I dared not say out loud: are our churches also broken? As the correctional system is expected to rehabilitate but is failing to hit its mark, are our churches, designed to build faith, also missing their mark, producing instead churchgoers with a limited connection to God?

The feeling engulfed me, ceasing to release its grip.

The reflex muscles contracted around the imaginary towel in my throat, trying to push out the blockage. I'm standing in quicksand, knowing if I stay here, I will die, but yet I stay. Why? What is pushing me to hold on to what is ineffective in my life? At that moment, the church had become a mere holding ground for my faithlessness. My faith was not being built, but harnessed. Merely held together. Not being stretched, but cajoled. I was flattered by admiring glances and stares. I willingly stayed because it was safer than the outside world. I stayed because it was somehow comforting. I stayed because it was familiar. What I didn't hear myself saying was that I stayed because of Christ.

Then I heard Him softly whisper, "Relationship." The problem and the answer, you see, wasn't the church. It was me. I was searching but because I didn't know what I was searching for, I fell prey to whatever made me feel good at the moment. Then grew discontent when it didn't fill the void I yearned to fill. I had latched on to church, but it was a shallow substitute for a true relationship with the Savior.

*"It is for freedom that Christ has set us free. Stand firm, then, and do not let yourself be burdened again by a yolk of slavery." (Gal. 5:1)*

Every family has its mode of operation, mostly an unwritten law of things, like what happens in the family stays in the family. You don't air the family's dirty laundry. We spend the rest of our lives adjusting to these laws from which we should be free. Something that constrained us twenty years earlier still grips us and shows itself in our families today. Being bound is powerful because the imprisonment is not only physical but mental and emotional.

Food was a scarcity in my house growing up. We were a hard-working, lower-class family. Dad worked long hard hours at the steel mill, which eventually claimed his voice years later to cancer. Mom worked the 11-7 nursing shift at the hospital and applied hair and makeup on the deceased at the local funeral home on the weekends. We lived in a small two-bedroom, one-bath house with eight people. Mom and Dad had their bedroom, and the girls and boys rotated turns in the other.

When the girls had the bedroom, I shared the bed with all my sisters. But during the off times, my bed was three chairs pushed together in the dining room area nearest the fan. Throw down some blankets and a pillow off the couch, and life was good. My brother's favorite spot was under the table. Crazy when I think about it now, but the point is, everyone made do. It was our family's mode of operation. The funny thing is we never realized that things were bad until someone else pointed it out. My dad eventually was able to scrounge up enough money for a permit to turn the garage into a bedroom, and we became a three-bedroom family. We had hit the lottery! Mom and Dad took the garage, the boys had their room, and the girls ours.

Some of my greatest memories were formed living in that wonderful little house. Saturday night family sing-offs, long before *The Voice* and *American Idol*. The girls would break out in song with The Supremes and the boys would answer with the Temptations. To this day when I travel home, I always drive by that little house, just to see it, to remember the little box that contains my childhood.

But we built around our circumstances and create our reality. Life as I knew it was as normal as could be because everyone else around me was in similar situations.

Similarly, in an attempt to create normal in my adult, crazy, out-of-control life, I found myself with a duty-bound faith. One that I did out of habit and obligation but did not feed me or help me grow. I had boxed myself in, just as with the little house where I grew up, in an ill-fitting dwelling that I didn't realize existed until I walked down the steps of the church that day.

This chapter is designed to make you squirm a little. To ask hard questions about things that you've been conditioned to accepted as normal. Has church become habitual? Is your relationship with God routine? Have you built around family dysfunction and are left wondering why you aren't thriving?

We go through this life building toward the afterlife. We read God's word, give God praise and glory for the good and the bad in our lives, but our understanding is limited.

*"For now we see only a reflection as in a mirror; then we shall see face to face. Now I know in part; then I shall know fully, even as I am fully known." (I Cor. 13:12)*

44

God took me to the edge of the cliff on the steps of the church that day to show me what I already knew, but had refused to see. Salvation and celebrity had intersected many times before only to be brushed off as no big deal. I felt myself panic, begin to emotionally scramble, and somehow try to figure out a way to alter His direction for my life. When He says it's time to move, then it's time to move, no matter how uncertain you may feel. That walk to the car felt like forever as "If I don't go back, now what?" played over and over in my head.

Journalist Finley Peter Dunne coined a phrase: "God came to disturb the comfortable and to comfort the disturbed," and I was growing increasingly more uncomfortable. He was like an eagle pushing me out of the nest I no longer fit in.

My mom was a master of creating something out of nothing. We ate beans in so many varieties that you wouldn't know they were beans if she didn't tell you. We called her the queen of disguise. One day God deliberately shook things up in the Jefferson household. There was nothing to disguise. The many jobs had produced all that it could and left things lacking. I recall that morning clearly. Usually, in our leanest times, we ate sugar sandwiches (yep, just as it sounds—wet the bread just enough for the sugar to adhere, fold it in half, and magic!) but on this day, I remember leaving for school with nothing but a promise: "I'll bring lunch by lunchtime."

As the day went on, I kept looking at the clock on the wall, knowing that lunchtime was approaching. My stomach rumbled, reminding me that I had nothing to eat. The bell rang and everyone rushed out to lunch. What do you do? You suck it up, put on a brave face, and pretend you're not hungry. My little sister and I were on the playground, climbing on the fence (something you could never do today), and we saw our mom coming up the sidewalk, clutching her tattered coat with two paper bag lunches. We ran toward her. She handed our lunches over the fence, and after a few brief love yous, she disappeared the way she came.

Kids asked, "Who was that? Was that your mom?"

I sat on the ground, alone, far away from nosey kids with prying eyes, opened my bag, and inside found a baggie with a scrambled egg and two slices of canned cling peaches. I ate in tears that day, but not for the reason you may think.

I had been exposed. Embarrassed. Everyone saw my mom in that tattered coat bring that little bag of nothing. God had kicked over my box, and I was angry. How could she do this to me? How could God let her do this to me? Even though He had provided, my concern, even at age ten, was how things looked to others. I was blind to what God, through my mom, had done.

We find throughout scripture that Jesus was always kicking over man-made boxes. His opposition was not out of a lack of love for His creation, but rather love to break us out of what binds our faith.

*"Are you so foolish after beginning with the Spirit are you now trying to attain your goal by human efforts." (Gal 3:3)*

My little faith had begun to put stock in my mom's ability to work magic. After all, she could do the impossible, rather than God's grace. To this day, I don't know how she came up with eggs and a can of peaches, but it filled the stomachs of her babies that morning. A small gesture. But for me, it was a foreshadowing of what was to come: me putting my faith in the ability of man over God. Years later, with kids of my own, the scales of blindness have fallen off my eyes and a deep welling up of gratitude overtakes me, one that my little heart couldn't possibly grasp at the time.

Jesus, it often seemed, opposed the Pharisees, the religious watchdogs, because of their misplaced hope. They trusted more in their righteousness and ability rather than His grace. The things He did, how He did them, even when He did them (like my ten-year-old self) made them angry rather than grateful. They were angry because Jesus embarrassed them with "His way." On that day, I'm ashamed to say, He embarrassed me.

In my young mind, my mom must have been angry at us. I don't know for what, but surely there was something. We were always in trouble, so there were a plethora of things to choose from. Jumping on the beds, breaking a window, you name it. Even living in poverty, you see, my mom was very particular about her appearance, so to show up looking a mess had to be intentional, mean, and purposeful. It strayed from what I was accustomed to. Just as the Pharisees reasoned that Jesus had an atrial motive other than love because He obviously was not of God to heal on the Sabbath. My limited understanding could not compute such a gesture of sacrifice. Likewise, I find myself bringing Christ down to the size of my limited understanding, rather than stretching my understanding to meet His brilliance. Leaving Him but one choice: to kick over my box.

As much as I love my mom, in that isolated moment, I was more concerned about the protocol than the relationship. You arrive early and leave an appropriate lunch at the front office. That's how it was done. Certainly not late and in view for all to see, dressed like *that*! Etiquette had overtaken kinship and in full view of everyone, just as with the Pharisees, Jesus had kicked my box over. In other words, exposed me for who I really was.

Inside I raged. "Who do you think you are?" was my silent response toward my mom. I can only imagine how I made her feel that day. I felt justified, even vindicated, that she felt bad. She should have left crying. What she did was wrong. An oppressed, stunted faith allows you to say out loud or secretly in your hearts, "I didn't ask Jesus to die for me. Now He wants to embarrass me by showing up in my life expecting submission and obedience? He should cry." Harsh words, I know, and deliberately so. I needed to be shaken up. Jolted, as a defibrillator frantically being applied to save my life. Self-pity had a tight grip, and life had given me lots of reasons to be justified. I had become immune to my spiritual condition, lulled into a state of complacency. I was bound by a false security blanket that, because life had been hard, somehow God owed me something.

I recall my initial response to John 5, the healing at the pool when Jesus asked the man who had been an invalid for thirty-eight years, *"Do you want to get well?"*

Sometime later, Jesus went up to Jerusalem for one of the Jewish festivals. ² Now there is in Jerusalem near the Sheep Gate a pool, which in Aramaic is called Bethesda and which is surrounded by five covered colonnades. ³ Here a great number of disabled people used to lie—the blind, the lame, the paralyzed. One who was there had been an invalid for thirty-eight years. When Jesus saw him lying there and learned that he had been in this condition for a long time, He asked him, "Do you want to get well?"

"Sir," the invalid replied, "I have no one to help me into the pool when the water is stirred. While I am trying to get in, someone else goes down ahead of me."

Then Jesus said to him, "Get up! Pick up your mat and walk."

I thought, what a jerk. How rude. Of course he wants to get well. Why would you even ask that? My enabling, codependent broken child wrapped herself around this broken man almost protecting him. You see, I too had set up residence in my brokenness. This question threatened my existence. Jesus wasn't just speaking to the invalid, but to me. *BJ, do you want to get well?*

Now a mom myself, I know the sting of shame having unintentionally embarrassed my children. I know the bitter pill she had to swallow to walk away in silence. The walk home had to be a tearful one. Anguishing over not being able to provide more and make her kids proud. I don't recall the playground conversation after she left, but the abandonment echoed loudly with every fading step as her figure slowly disappeared down the street.

I shiver at the number of times Jesus must have walked that same walk of pain. Disowned by me. Chess is a game of skill and strategy that most never master. Yet on a daily basis, I challenged God, the Creator of the world, in a game of chess. And like the Pharisees, with all of their wisdom and great intention, I was fighting a losing battle.

Decades later, I can now look back and see the masterful hand of the Maker chiseling away at the facade of my life. At the core of who I am, I am an actor, a hypocrite. I wear many faces and play many roles. I now realize I wasn't a young girl trying to find her way back to the Father. He never left me. Rather I was a young girl trying to find herself so that she could be reintroduced to the Father in earnest and truth. What I once saw as public humiliation and shame was His breaking the hold of others' opinions in my life.

I went through a divorce in full view of my church community. I was one who touted that God hates divorce and they never happened in His kingdom. I was deeply challenged! Shame and embarrassment enveloped me. What matters most: God's opinion or man's?

I suffered the loss of a child, which temporarily left me emotionally incapacitated, long before seeking therapy was acceptable in the church because God alone should be enough. I was deeply challenged! What matters most: His opinion or man's?

I suffered ministry firings under the jeering eyes of those who once supported me but now deemed me unfit to lead. I was deeply challenged! What matters most, God's opinion or man's?

He was kicking over my box. My box of people-pleasing and craving the acceptance of man. I'd rebuild it, and He'd kick it over again until I finally gave up the fight and surrendered. God, You alone are enough!

What about you? What box of yours is He continuously kicking over? Desire to fit in? To be lifted up and praised? To be publicly acknowledged? What matters most, God's opinion or man's?

Jesus opposed the Pharisees over their traditions and their self-righteous stand for rules rather than a relationship with Him.

What traditions are you hiding behind? What binds you?

Truthfully, I don't know if God is really going to care, when we are face to face, about how many times we've read through the Bible from beginning to end. I'm not sure that knowing what the scriptures say in Greek or Latin is going to place us closer in line with Jesus. I don't even know if He will care if we were Catholic, Protestant, or Baptist during our time here on Earth. It never seems to come up in scripture. What does surface time and again is whether or not we know Him and do His will.

*"Not everyone who says to me, 'Lord, Lord', will enter the kingdom of heaven, but only he who does the will of my Father who is in heaven."*
*Matthew 7:21*

Maybe it's time to look at your spiritual journey. What do you see? What is the condition of your faith? After a long, hard examination, I found I was bound in a box that Jesus was continually kicking over, only to be rebuilt by me as a stronger fortress.

I don't know about you, but I'm not that smart so He made His word understandable to unschooled, ordinary people like me *(Acts 2:13)*. I'm not that loving so He gave grace and mercy to the unlovable sinner like me *(Rom. 3:24)*. I'm not that awesome so He stooped low to make me great *(Ps. 18:35)*. That gives me hope because I don't have to be perfect to serve Him, but I have to be free.

Unbound, our individual walks will be completely unrecognizable to all around us. Maybe that is the point...like John the Baptist, for us to decrease so that He can increase! Imagine what this world would look like if we actually allowed God to do what He does best...*be God!*

## NAKED REFLECTION

### Theme Scripture: Hebrew 4: 16

*"Let us then approach God's throne of grace with confidence, so that we may receive mercy and find grace to help us in our time of need."*

**Prayer:** Father, I want to know You and be known by You. You created me in my mother's womb. You know every hair on my head and every thought before it is formed on my tongue. Nothing about me is hidden from You. Let me stand before You in confidence even in my brokenness. Remove from me anything that separates me from You so that we can be one as the Father and the Son are one. In Jesus' name, Amen.

## NAKED STUDY

The strength of an NBA rebounder is in their ability to go after the ball every time and not give up until they have the ball in their hands. The difference between a good rebounder and a great rebounder is determination. This Naked Reflection is to test your Rebound IQ. How bad do you want it, and to what extent are you willing to go to change?

**Q.** Stuck in my desire to please people even to my own spiritual detriment I stayed in a church that didn't serve me until God forced a move. What box(es) are you confined to, and how has it stunted your growth?

_____

_____

_____

_____

_____

_____

**Q.** Examine your life. What is one area that God is calling you to surrender to Him that you are still holding on to?

_____

_____

_____

_____

_____

_____

**Q.** What keeps you from letting go?

_____

_____

_____

_____

_____

**Q.** Truthfully, we build houses around our brokenness. How has holding on to what God is calling you to release, negatively and positively, served you?

_____

_____

_____

_____

_____

_____

# 5

## SILENCED LAMBS

Growing up I was always afraid of my own shadow. I was afraid of trying, afraid of failing, afraid of succeeding, afraid of getting caught, afraid of being forgotten, afraid of being remembered. I was the one who faded into the woodwork, afraid of the imaginary ghost that loomed in my mind but extended into my reality. To this day my siblings tease me about being so afraid that I hid behind a door, but because I gripped the doorknob, they could see the door shaking. Fear so ridiculous that it's almost funny—until it's not.

I recall a family car ride with my dad and us kids. As we were cruising down the road, I noticed a police car following us with its lights flashing. I was on my knees, facing the rear of the car, watching (this was before the seat belt laws of today). I watched them, and they watched me. I turned and looked toward the front seat then turned back and looked at them. This continued for about two blocks until I turned and sat down, occasionally glancing over my shoulder at them, and then they finally turned on the siren. At that time, my dad realized they were there and pulled over.

The first thing they asked my dad was "Didn't you see us following you? Why didn't you pull over when we first signaled you?"

My dad's response: "Sorry, I didn't see you, officer."

"Well, didn't your little girl tell you we were there?"

"No, sir," he said. "She did not."

I shiver when I replay that scene in my mind, knowing now what I couldn't possibly have known then. The danger we encountered because of my silence. A black man in the South, in the '60s, not pulling over for two white cops. Stories of beatings, lynchings, and mysterious disappearances besiege my mind, yet by the grace of God it turned out well. A tail light needing repair and two white officers with a heart. When I look back, I wonder what kept me from speaking. I knew instantly what I should do. I knew we hadn't done anything wrong. I knew my dad hadn't seen the cops, but as my heart raced and my mind grew cloudy, I became mute, unable to utter a sound.

At that moment, I stood face to face with fear, and the lamb had been silenced. Fear—life's greatest crippler.

If this had been one isolated incident, I could chalk it up to childhood uncertainty. My school transcript, however, is riddled with trips to the principal's office for perceived silent acts of defiance. I was even kicked out of the youth choir because I wouldn't sing. I became apt at swallowing my words as a defense mechanism. Protecting myself from the meanness of the world by never putting myself on the cutting block.

Unfortunately, I, and probably like some of you, carried this mode of protection into our spiritual lives as well. Afraid that God, like the officers, is somehow out to get us. He won't listen, has His mind made up, or worse yet, doesn't care. If we remain silent, we can somehow go undetected and hide under the radar. Like the little girl riding in the car, we know what we should do, but we question if He will find fault in our execution of it. We've done nothing, at least at that moment, wrong, but surely there are many other wrongs in which we are very much at fault. So instead of laying ourselves on the spiritual line, we purposefully remain silent, hiding in the shadow.

Sounds like a sensible thing to do, right? No one wants to get shot down. Unfortunately, "when you shut others out, you shut yourself in." I found myself trapped behind my wall of protection. I even stopped speaking for a period of my life. Deliberately. I wrote everything down and pretended to be Blind, like my grandmother. Somehow, I felt safe and found comfort in it. Growing up in a large family made it easy to go undetected as everyone was trying to find their space. So, I grew to love the me that no one could see.

But now here we are as adults in this large family of God, trying to find our place with a mechanism of shutdown that does not serve us. I found myself blending into the woodwork, occasionally poking my head out for a quick gulp of survival air, afraid that I may say the wrong thing to the wrong people. Afraid I may not be able to live up to the demands and expectations placed upon me. Afraid I might fail God. Afraid of my own sinful nature. Afraid of others' opinions about me.

My voice, like any muscle you've ceased to exercise, had gone into a state of atrophy. It had to be rediscovered, redeveloped, and redefined, beginning with what shut it down in the first place, which is:

## FEAR THAT GOD WILL SEE ME FOR WHO I REALLY AM AND CHANGE HIS MIND ABOUT LOVING ME!

So, we hide! It's a common theme in scripture:
- "He answered, 'I heard you in the garden, and I was afraid because I was naked; *so I hid.*'" Genesis 3:10
- "He said also, 'I am the God of your father, the God of Abraham, the

God of Isaac, and the God of Jacob.' Then Moses *hid his face*, for he was afraid to look at God." Exodus 3:6

- ""Can a man *hide himself* in secret places so that I cannot see him?' declares the Lord. 'Do I not fill heaven and earth?' declares the Lord." Jeremiah 23:24
- "Now I, Daniel, alone saw the vision, while the men who were with me did not see the vision; nevertheless, a great dread fell on them, and they *ran away to hide themselves*." Daniel 10:7
- "So I was afraid and *went out and hid* your gold in the ground." Matthew 25:25

He had intentionally been placing me in difficult situations to force me to exercise my atrophied muscle. Finally admitting the truth that I was hiding from God, the master-builder could begin His good work, the convergence of the gifts He had given me to speak and to teach with the thorn in my flesh, fear of being myself. Like Paul in II Cor. 12:7-10, this was my thorn in my flesh to show that God's grace was sufficient for me. *Because of these surpassingly great revelations. Therefore, in order to keep me from becoming conceited, I was given a thorn in my flesh, a messenger of Satan, to torment me.[8] Three times I pleaded with the Lord to take it away from me.[9] But he said to me, "My grace is sufficient for you, for my power is made perfect in weakness." Therefore I will boast all the more gladly about my weaknesses, so that Christ's power may rest on me.[10] That is why, for Christ's sake, I delight in weaknesses, in insults, in hardships, in persecutions, in difficulties. For when I am weak, then I am strong.* Bringing about, for the first time in my life, true confidence over cowardice, solid convictions rather than hypocrisy, He was developing a vessel He could use albeit stored in this jar of clay.

We've all had crazy things said and done to us in the name of religion, things that would make your head spin. I've sat silent over many disturbing internal church struggles, enduring many unholy opinions and attitudes and hierarchies of righteousness. I'm convinced the church will forever be flawed because it's made up of flawed people. There were many things I should have spoken up about and fought for, but you can't go to battle unarmed. I had to first find my voice or fall prey to the loudest or strongest opinion in the room. My voice had been silenced for years, not by a church, but by the weakness of my underdeveloped relationship with God. A relationship built on punishment rather than trust. Chastisement rather than encouragement. Fear rather than faith. I had to return to the scene of the crime, the crucial starting point. Like with the domino effect, if the first piece is not properly placed, it doesn't matter how long or elaborately you build it. It will not work.

We all grow up with natural fears that serve as exercises for overcoming. I failed most but overcame some. More importantly, I developed a propensity to rely on my own feeble strength because I *feared* relying on God. After all, someday He would find out I was not worthy of that love. Satan is very predictable. He is the father of lies, but this time I was equipped to do battle God's way, having put on the *full* armor of God. In my haste to dress myself, I had neglected to put on a basic foundational garment: the belt of truth. Truth about who God was in relation to me: my protector, not my enemy; my deliverer, not my oppressor; my redeemer, not my betrayer.

Nothing with God is ever wasted, but simple strokes of color in His vibrant masterpiece. Growing up in poverty made me tenuous, dark experiences revealed the warrior, life successes gave me confidence, and faith struggles were my road to humility. Now I see clearly what before I only saw in part; faith in crisis is faith in development. It's where the master does His greatest work.

Although his tactics vary, Satan's goal is the same: *to silence the lamb.*

We see it in Matt. 4:1-11 with the Temptation of Jesus. *Then Jesus was led by the Spirit into the wilderness to be tempted by the devil. 2 After fasting forty days and forty nights, he was hungry.3 The tempter came to him and said, "If you are the Son of God, tell these stones to become bread."*

Unable even in death to silence the Lamb of God, what better tactic than to attack and silence the little lambs left behind. It is no coincidence that Jesus calls Peter to feed and care for His lambs. We are fragile, easily misguided, performance-driven, insecure sheep, wandering through a maze we don't know how to maneuver. Too prideful to ask for direction, we gravitate toward those who appear knowledgeable and follow. Unfortunately, Satan always camouflages himself as knowledgeable. Knowledgeable on the goodness (or lack thereof) of God toward His creation. He knows the importance of the first domino: belief that God loves and accepts me (blemishes and all), no matter what!

Satan's creed:

If I can get you to DOUBT God, I can get you to FEAR God.

If I can get you to FEAR God, I can get you to DISTRUST God.

If I can get you to DISTRUST God, I can get you to LEAVE God!

## NAKED REFLECTION

### Theme Scripture: Isaiah 12: 2

*"Surely God is my salvation; I will trust and not be afraid. The LORD, the LORD himself, is my strength and my defense; he has become my salvation."*

**Prayer:** *God, I'm tired of hiding from You. Our union has been built around my weaknesses and shortcomings afraid to bring them to You. I know I can't have a deep relationship with You unless I'm willing to give You all of me. You already know the things I am afraid to admit. Help me to have the courage to go beyond being a spiritual acquaintance to a trusting, loving relationship with You built on truth and honesty. In Jesus' name, amen.*

My younger sister is everything I am not: open, free-spirited, self-assured. She would always go to Dad to ask for money, come back with a quarter, and off to the corner store we'd go. Once, she headed in for her weekly routine and came back with her shiny quarter, but this time I asked her to go back and get one for me. My dad, in his brilliance, had noticed that I never asked for anything myself. His response to my sister changed the trajectory of my little life that day.

He said, "If your sister wants something from me, she needs to come ask me herself." It took the wind out of me when she came back with those words. It took a few minutes before I mustered up the courage to do it, but I did.

His words: "I love you. Do you think I would give to your sister and not give to you?" They were prophetic words spoken to the heart of a frightened little girl.

My dad had never given me a reason to be afraid of him, but I was. He was the breadwinner, the disciplinarian, the rule setter. He kept our house running smoothly, and when I look back, I was afraid, with so many children, that he couldn't love me too.

Have you placed limits on God's ability to love us all and you in particular?

## NAKED STUDY

**Q.** Without judging yourself as to whether or not it's true, what frightens you about God?

_____

_____

_____

_____

_____

**Q.** What have you ceased to ask God for?

_____

_____

_____

_____

_____

**Q.** How does your crippling fear show itself in your life?

_____

_____

_____

_____

_____

**Q.** If the domino effect determines the finished product, what is the condition of your first domino (your faith)?

_____

_____

_____

_____

_____

_____

**Q.** What part of Satan's creed trips you up the most? Doubt? Fear? Distrust? And why?

_____

_____

_____

_____

_____

_____

# NOTES

# 6

## DROWNING IN THE WHITE NOISE OF RELIGION

I can't swim! But that never stopped me on hot summer days from grabbing one of my mom's good towels (which was never wise) and heading to the pool with my brothers. They were the cute boys who all the girls liked to watch dive off the high board. My little sister and I were just tagalongs because they were our babysitters for the day. Not a bad solution, except I couldn't swim, which meant I was a pest in the water. So, at the age of eight, my brother decided to remedy that problem. In our community pool, full of excited swimmers and lifeguards, into the deep end of the pool he threw me. Soon my instinct would kick in, and I would start to swim, or at least float. Or so he thought.

Like a movie playing in slow motion, I vividly recall the scene. The cold splash of the water engulfed my body as I descended rapidly, eyes wide open, frightfully aware of the sea of bodies bobbing all around. The muffled sounds of screams and laughter while frantically ingesting gulps of water as I descended into the deep and hit the pool floor. Then my fade into darkness. All the while my internal voice was screaming, "I CAN'T SWIM!" I was surrounded by throngs of people yet no one noticed that a child went down and hadn't come up.

My next awareness was of someone frantically pumping my stomach, saying, "Come on, come on, spit it out."

Spring forward many years later. It's amazing how the body remembers. As I wrote these words, my heart began to speed up, my breathing became shallow, and my hands began to shake. Muscle recall from an event so long ago thrust me back into my greatest childhood fear...drowning. The terror of slowly fading, screaming for help with so many within hearing range, but not being heard. Flailing to get air while those around me bobbed with carefree abandon.

Childhood fears sometimes grow up to become adult terrors. This near-drowning sensation has occurred so many times in my adult life that it became a new normal. To the pool, I went on my own accord. The cool, sparkling water offered a welcome break from the crazy world around me. The throngs of familiar faces became an extended family with a common purpose, a place where you were accepted even if your swimsuit was old or you were a little overweight. My new normal, however, was no longer the waters of a swimming pool, but the once-sacred walls of a church where I often found myself drowning in the white noise of religion. Desperately reaching for safety but feeling pulled by the undercurrent deeper into an abyss.

Now, as I approach this chapter, hear me when I say I'm a church girl! Grew up in it and will, no doubt, die in it. I cherish being lifted in praise to the rafters of heaven as the whole body sings, "Holy, Holy, Holy." Being collectively ushered into the presence of the Almighty transforms my soul. My spirit yearns for it! Church, the body of Christ, is as precious to me as the breath of my children. But here I sit today asking, God...are You there? There's so much happening around me. So much coming at me that I can't find you.

My oldest brother was one of the most talented, smartest, caring people I'd ever known, but over the years, drugs slowly robbed him of all of that. Having spent most of his adult life in and out of jail, locked up for petty crimes, being institutionalized became a mindset. Nonetheless, I was ecstatic because my big brother was finally coming home. I recall the excitement, the jubilation, and the anxiety of seeing him again after nearly twenty years. What would he be like? Will prison have hardened him? Would he still remember our crazy childhood stories with the same throw-your-head-back, laugh-until-you-cry glee?

I just didn't know what to expect because, you see, the carefree boy I knew at nineteen was now coming home, a man, nearly forty years old. So much life had happened in those missed years. Think about it: life as he'd known it had completely changed. In the span of those twenty years, we now had personal computers, CD players, cell phones (although they were huge), DNA fingerprinting, everything disposable, from diapers to cameras to contact lenses, and even games we could take with us in the Nintendo Gameboy. Things we had grown into, he was seeing for the first time, and his mind was blown. We see it in a movie, and it's funny watching people experience these things anew, but in real life, it doesn't quite play out that way. It's overwhelming. All their senses short-circuit inside of them, trying rapidly to grab on and make sense of it all.

We live in an overstimulated society. No wonder we are always in a state of anxiety. As a backup vocalist, I have toured the world performing with some of the greatest recording artists. Every town, as beautifully spectacular as they were, became the same. Hours of rehearsing. It wasn't so much the vocals that consumed us—that was the easy part—but rather the production of it all. I can tell you little to nothing about the Eiffel Tower, or Big Ben, Niagara Falls, Germany, or Johannesburg, even though I've spent time in them all. Concerts, you see, are no longer just about the voice of the singer, but the lighting, stage production, pyrotechnics, and all of the media blitz surrounding them. People are looking to be entertained, mesmerized, snatched away from reality. And this is true not just on the entertainment stage, but in everyday life and in churches as well. Because of that, we find ourselves competing for the "biggest and best" award. But if you ask any singer what they prefer, you will hear, nine times out of ten, the intimacy of a small venue where they get to simply sing and connect heart to heart with the audience.

My brother loved life and easily jumped back into the things that brought him joy: cooking, singing, serving other people, taking classes to get his degree so that he could get a decent job, which is quite a bit harder to do when you have "convicted felony" before your name and a monitoring bracelet around your ankle. But he was doing it with ease. Or so it appeared. In hindsight, we should have taken more care of his mental health, his mental adjustment back into society, but you don't think about such things. Or at least we didn't. Then one day, what seemed like out of the blue, he took a gun and walked across the bridge to the nearest police station. After nearly two decades in prison and less than a year on the outside, like a scene out of *The Shawshank Redemption*, he decided it was all too much, being a husband to someone you've only communicated with through letters, a father to nearly grown kids that he held as a baby, but nothing more. Walking in with his hands held high, he loudly announced. "I'm a parolee and I have an unloaded gun in my pocket," knowing that having a weapon would be breaking his parole, ensuring jail time. He wanted to go back, back to what was simpler, back to what was familiar.

My brother's situation, I realize, was an extreme one, but I believe there is something to be learned from it. I can't tell you how many times I've sat in churches, overstimulated, overloaded, and wanting nothing more than to go back to something simpler. Bigger isn't always better. I love music, but the church is not where I go to be entertained. I love lights, but don't let it blind me to the word. I was watching the children's choir perform one Sunday morning when it all became crystal clear. Their beautiful, little, angelic and not so angelic voices, upstaged by the flashiness of the moment. We all rose in a standing ovation as they hammed it up for us, and we egged them on. It was cute and funny and adorable. What it wasn't was pure and God-centered. A small, amusing moment of enjoyment for us, I know, but this is the foundation for them. That's when it hit me that we are doing a disservice to ourselves and them in the long run. I longed for the time when kids could sing, "Jesus loves Me," and we didn't need floating hearts and flying angels across the stage to be moved to our feet. Sheer distractions from a world already full of distractions. I think what I longed for most was to be grounded.

*"And I pray that you, being rooted and established in love, may have power, together with all the Lord's holy people, to grasp how wide and long and high and deep is the love of Christ, and to know this love that surpasses knowledge—that you may be filled to the measure of all the fullness of God."*
*Eph. 3:17-19*

These are the times I found myself drowning in the white noise. I know I'm about to date myself, but believe it or not, there was a time when TV signed off, unlike today, where we have around-the-clock programming. At midnight, they'd play the national anthem, salute the flag, and then signed off to reset for the next day. Now, if you were rebellious like me, sometimes you'd try to stay up later looking for a random program, but all you found was static because the transmitter had been turned off. That white noise after a short period, because nothing is being disseminated, lulls you to sleep. In other words, nothing was being broadcast. At times, as a leader, I found myself talking but wondering if anything was being conveyed.

So, I had to ask myself, are we doing so much in God's churches *for* people that we're spiritually lulling them to sleep? Now, I'm not talking literally, although I've had my share of head-bobbing moments, but figuratively. In teaching, we have the "I do, we do, you do" principle.

It's first "let me show you how to do it," then "let us do it together," and then the final step, which is where we grow most, the "let me see you do it." The kids hate this part because this is where they have to struggle through. Where they run out of eraser. They'd much rather you do the work for them. We're all, not just kids, built that way. I had to learn that my intimacy with God can only be developed by me trying and messing up, trying and messing up, and trying again. It could not be manufactured, no matter how good the intent, and served up on a plate for me to enjoy.

That kind of intimacy only comes through the struggle. Flailing at the bottom of the swimming pool, I was learning to fight to survive, the exact lesson I would have to grab onto decades later. You see, if I was going to be a Christian in the entertainment industry, I had to learn to fight. Fight to hear the Father directing me over all the other noise competing for my headspace. Everywhere I turned, there was a new battle, some large, some small. But here is where the young warrior learns to conquer. The clothes you would or would not wear because they were too revealing. The drugs you would or would not do to fit in. The people you would or would not sleep with to advance your career. Truth is, the white noise, the talk of God but lack of relationship with Him, became the instrument Satan used to remove Him from His throne in my life. Like my brother, an addict, I had become hooked on church doing the God thing for me. Getting my fix Sunday to Sunday, but buckling under pressure during the week when real life came knocking.

Addicts do great when in rehab propped up and surrounded by ongoing support. The true test, however, is in the everyday. So, what do you do, CEO, when faced with pushing someone else down to make yourself look better? What do you do, student, when everyone else is cheating on a test you desperately need to pass but aren't quite sure you're ready for? What do you do, construction worker, when unfairly doubling the cost of labor will help get you out of debt sooner? What do you do when you realize you've ceased to develop your spiritual muscle, now that you need it most? Actress and singer aside, no matter who you are or what you do, the ability to stand firm under everyday pressures is learned in the trenches, not in the static.

It's weird, but it took a while before my brother realized I was drowning in the pool that day. I mean, you would think it would be instantaneous. At least that's how it plays out in my head. In movies, a drowning scene is pretty dramatic—the victim is thrashing about, desperately clinging to the last vestiges of life. However, real life is a lot different. You see, when people find themselves on the cusp of drowning, they enter a state of preservation, and the "instinctive drowning response" kicks in. That's when voluntary movement becomes impossible, and the person tends to bob listlessly with their head thrown back and mouth level with the water. The eyes may be glassy or altogether closed but, surprisingly, the legs do not kick, and the arms are held against the body. The instinctive drowning response is so undramatic that people often succumb even with lifeguards and other swimmers around. Whoa, this blew my mind, because I recognized that for years, I had been experiencing a spiritual dry drowning and never even saw it coming. There I was, bobbing listlessly (going through the motions), eyes glassy (seeing, but not seeing), in a state of preservation (safeguarding). In other words, going to church, but getting little to nothing out of it that would sustain me. Again, hear me when I say that I am not anti-church. But I am anti-dying, and if I was going to survive, I needed to do something different.

As terrifying as it was, my brother made a bold move that day walking into a police station with an unloaded gun. He could have easily been shot and killed, and rightfully so. But that day, grace and mercy showed on him as they wrestled him to the floor while sobbing, "I want to go back." Instead of punishment, they got him to a hospital and gave him the help he needed. When I found myself, likewise, disconnected from the Father, crying inside, "I want to go back," I had to first stop punishing myself with the "what's wrong with you" line of questioning. Everyone else loves it here, so what's your problem? The music is fantastic, are you kidding me? Oh, you're just being a diva, get over yourself. A church full of thousands can't possibly be wrong. For a while, I berated myself incessantly, trying to make me fit into the equation. But then I grasped that it was less about the church and more about me. The church offered to some exactly what they needed. If it was not feeding me, I needed to find a church home that spoke to my soul, whether it was among thousands or ten. You see, for years I just went with the flow, not making waves, waiting for someone else to fix what was broken in me. But at some point, you are called to decide for yourself and refuse to be a victim.

Martin Luther King, Jr. has a powerful, less repeated quote that since I was a child I've loved. Now I've come to know why it resonated so. "Whenever men and women straighten their backs up, they're going somewhere because a man can't ride your back unless it is bent." I had been walking through life bent over. Standing tall in my professional life, but bent in my spiritual and personal life. Eventually, your back begins to break and you reach a point when questioning ends, and instead, like Peter, you have to do something bold.

*"Then the disciple whom Jesus loved said to Peter, "It is the Lord!" As soon as Simon Peter heard him say, "It is the Lord," he wrapped his outer garment around him (for he had taken it off) and jumped into the water."*
*John 21:7*

Shortly after the crucifixion of Jesus, Peter, caught up in the hurt and disappointment of his grief, went to where he had gone many times before: his boat. It was, no doubt, his safe place. The place he goes to clear his head. The place he goes not to think. He invited no one to come along, although the others joined him anyway. Surrounded by the undulating motion of the water and the droning voices of the others also in mourning around him, we see him being lulled into self-preservation mode. Safeguarding his heart. Then John, the disciple Jesus loved, shook him into reality by announcing, "It is the Lord." The Lord, whom Peter had pledged his life to, but had so quickly failed. The one he found himself disconnected from but desperately wanted to go back to. So, at that moment, he did something no one else on board would do. He did something bold. Instead of waiting for the Lord to come to him, he went to the Lord. He jumped out of the comfort of his boat.

I've made some bold moves in my life, but nothing like what this would require. A country girl from Texas braving the bright lights of New York City's Broadway stage, saying no to prominent movie roles because of principle, walking away from Hollywood at the peak of my career against agents' and managers' advice, traveling the world to war-filled countries where they were burning flags and shouting, "Americans, get out!", rebuilding my life from scratch after years in an abusive marriage… the list goes on. Others around me would say, "No one perseveres like BJ," and labeled me as courageous. For years, I believed it and wore it like a banner as proof of my love and devotion to God, but truthfully, as I've said before, I am a coward! The banner I wore brought me praise and adoration from man, but I was a poor reflection of God. You see, for years, I was afraid to vacate the safety of my spiritual boat for fear of going it alone. Seeing Jesus in the distance, even hearing, "It is the Lord," but insisting that He come to me rather than I to Him. After all, what would people say? What if I sink before reaching Him? What if those in the boat are right and I am wrong? Cowards can always find a reason *not* to do something. Today, I'm asking you to look at your reason *to* do something. His name is Jesus!

When you see the face of Jesus, are you willing to leave the others behind to get to the God of truth? To quiet all the noise around you and sit in silence at the Master's feet?

I needed a reality check. You see, I was so busy doing Godlike things, studying the Bible with people, evangelizing the world, teaching Sunday school, addressing women at conferences, and the like, that I drowned out God with my words and actions. My religious activities were just white noise of distraction. I was so convinced that I was following His teachings that I found myself arguing with God to maintain my status quo. *"God, I do love you with all my heart, mind, and soul. Can't you see that by all I'm doing for you?"* When confronted with the truth, I picked up stones to stone Him by getting angry. I called it hurt, but it was anger at God, and I pulled my heart away.

*"At this, they picked up stones to stone him, but Jesus hid himself, slipping away from the temple grounds." John 8: 59*

What about you? Are you needing to turn off the white noises of distraction in your life, whatever they may be, and refocus on the One that truly matters? If you get nothing else from this chapter, get this: having a disconnected phone cannot help us in a real emergency. We would think a person hilarious if talking into a dead phone when joking around, but insane if talking into a dead phone and his house was on fire. For some of us, our houses are on fire and we're talking into dead phones. I read a little book years ago that's probably no longer in publication called *I Refuse to Be a Victim*. It did two very important things for me: 1) it helped me admit that I had been living life as a victim, and 2) it called me to make the first move to change it.

It's time to get out of the boat!

In this time of standing for causes: #metoo, #blacklivesmatter, #pleasestand, and more, maybe it's time for a spiritual uprising of God's people, a movement of our own to take back God's church by taking back God's people. People willing to stand alone if necessary and say… #Nomore!

• No more praise and worship that rocks my body but doesn't anchor my soul.

- No more cool, hip sermons that make me laugh, but don't make me ponder change.
- No more rules and rituals making me appear holy before man, but far from God.
- No more titles making me holier than thou to sinners and untouchable to saints.
- No more casting stones at others to build my halo.
- No more avoiding the world God created out of fear that He can't protect me.
- No more judging the lives of others, while whitewashing my own.
- No more posturing over which churches are of God and which are not.
- No more filibustering over acceptable and unacceptable baptisms.
- No more nonsense over who are and who are not God's lost and saved children.

I don't know what it will take for you, but this was my starting point: getting to know Christ all over again and ridding myself of anything that blurred my view.

"I want to know Christ - *(the man, his heart, his message)*

And the power of his resurrection - *(the strength to rise up from the ashes of my dead life)* and the fellowship of sharing in his sufferings - *(joined in suffering with Christ) becoming like him in his death - (a reflection of His holiness),*" *(Phil. 3:10)*

I had to be courageous enough to ask myself...God, are You there?

If this is your journey and you find the answer is no, only you can answer why. Maybe it's:

- **A weak connection.** Are you too far away from the cell tower, God Himself?
- **A termination of services.** Have you failed to uphold your part of the contract?
- **An issue with the power supply.** Have you bothered to even charge the phone?

Jesus made it possible for us to have a connection to God that is crystal clear. No need to borrow someone else's phone or have someone call on your behalf. We would not tolerate the white noise of static on our cellphones for one day without beating down the doors of Verizon. Yet I went years without a clear connection to God and did nothing to change it.

How hard are you fighting? Are you willing to clear the way to get to Him? Sadly, for too long, my answer was no, and I continued to press *redial* and simply *hope* for a better connection next week rather than step out of the cycle of godlessness today.

Peter jumped out of the boat; Zacchaeus climbed high into a tree; the bleeding woman pushed through the crowd.

What are you willing to do?

## NAKED REFLECTION

Is it time to get off of the boat?
**Theme Scripture: John 8:31-32**

*"So He said to the Jews who had believed Him, "If you continue in My word, you are truly My disciples. Then you will know the truth, and the truth will set you free."*

**Prayer:** *Father, we are slaves to the familiar. We have become a nation of people who decorate around chaos. I beg you for a spirit of truth and honesty. Your word promises that the truth will set us free. Let us begin today with being truthful about what we see in ourselves and the chaos we call home around us.*

## NAKED STUDY

As a kid, I loved building houses out of cards. My brothers and sisters and I would challenge each other over who could build theirs the highest without falling. There were times when we'd spend hours building and pity the fool who would accidentally knock it over. Do you have any idea how much time and effort went into this construction that with the slightest breeze will go tumbling down? But I guarded it with every inch of my life. For all of my house of cards builders, are you guarding a house of cards that you already know is temporary, awaiting the slightest breeze, and everything you've invested is for naught?

Satan's greatest ploy is to get us to focus on the secondary rather than the primary. As children of God, we know that failing at the most important thing in this life (our walk with God) is not an option, but we often forsake it for the secondary honor of being accepted among the in-crowd.

Others may be able to skirt through, but what about you?

You may need to take many moments to pray before answering the following questions and/or solicit the unbiased eye of a *real* friend. The goal of this reflection is observatory, not critical, but it requires honesty, which we are unaccustomed to being with ourselves. Remember, we are where we are because we have convinced ourselves that everything is all right.

**Q.** What is the condition of those you have chosen to surround yourself with?

_____

_____

_____

_____

_____

John 5:3 "Here a great number of disabled people used to lie—the blind, the lame, the paralyzed."

This is a very familiar passage of scripture, and greater scholars than I have expounded the meaning. What I find frighteningly ironic is that they built a whole community around their condition. Some of us, not unlike the blind, the lame, and the paralyzed, have surrounded ourselves with others who are equally as incapacitated. On the one hand, it is comforting as we compare ourselves to others, but spiritually detrimental because it fails to call us out of the condition that binds us.

If your answer is unacceptable to you, then I ask:

Q. How long are you willing to languish there? Has their acceptance of you become more important than your spiritual well-being?

_____

_____

_____

_____

_____

John 5:5 "One who was there had been an invalid for thirty-eight years."

If a student remains in the same place academically, a teacher grows concerned. A mom, if her child ceases to eat or physically grow, runs immediately to a doctor. Yet as Christians, we give ourselves a pass to sit in spiritual limbo surprisingly for ten, twenty, thirty years. Surrounded by stained glass windows, choir robes, Christian sounding programs, and color-coded Bibles, we go through the motions in hopes it will be enough to get us to heaven. Why? We have become addicted to our affliction. We stay because it serves a purpose in our lives.

**Q.** What gratification/spiritual high are you getting from your affliction that permits you to willingly stay in your condition?

_____

_____

_____

_____

_____

_____

For years, my drug-addicted brother was a mystery to me. How can someone say they want change so passionately yet never break free? Through many words, tears, and countless interventions, the results were always the same…nothing. An addict is always chasing the high even though they know the high is temporary and that eventually, it will kill them. Some of us are religion junkies, and church is the drug we shoot into our arm every week. For a brief moment, it takes away all the pains of our life situations, but in actuality, it's creating a deeper hole from which many never climb out.

Q. What do you *need* to get well from?

_____

_____

_____

_____

_____

Q. What do you *want* to get well from?

_____

_____

_____

_____

Q. Is it time to leave all others behind and to get out of the boat?

_____

_____

_____

_____

_____

# 7

## BREATHE OR DIE

*"Finally the surgeon knelt beside his patient, and he took off his surgical mask and said, 'Mrs. Johnson, this is your surgeon. The operation went perfectly. Your heart has been repaired. Now tell your heart to beat again.' When he said that, the heart began to beat. When I heard this story, I thought I've got to write this song because there's so many people who have experienced so much brokenness to their heart. And even though God, the great surgeon, has saved us and repaired us, covered us with his grace, sometimes it takes you and me to tell our own heart to 'beat again, love again, hope again.'"*
*(The amazing story behind "Tell Your Heart to Breathe Again" by Randy (Phillips, Craig, and Dean)*

\*\*\*\*\*\*\*\*\*\*\*\*\*\*\*\*\*\*\*\*\*\*\*\*\*\*\*\*\*\*\*\*\*\*\*\*\*\*\*\*\*\*\*\*\*\*\*\*\*\*\*\*\*\*\*\*\*\*\*\*\*\*

The road back to anywhere can be a slow, tedious one. Even knowing where you're headed doesn't make the journey any easier or faster.

One day, I set out on a mission to walk to the shopping mall in the "other neighborhood." You see, our neighborhood didn't offer the same quality of stores that they did, and this was a special occasion—the prom—so I needed the best. Having traveled there in the car a couple of times, it seemed like a short distance. Surely, a track star could walk it. I started out giddy, carefree, and confident after mile one and mile two. But then came mile three, and mile four, and this outing didn't seem so worth it after all. I was hot, bothered, and bored (there was no listening to music on a cell phone back then). My feet were hurting, and the humidity in Texas is enough to send anyone running for cover. I kept telling myself that I had to be close—it must be right around this corner. But when it didn't appear around that corner, all bravado disappeared. I'd see a bus passing by and would contemplate hopping on the bus, but the frugal (I say frugal, my friends say cheap) side of me would say, "Girl, don't you waste that money. That's fifty cents you can use for something else." And the hopeful part of me kept saying, "But it's right around this corner. I'm sure of it." Then I'd find it wasn't.

Thoroughly ticked off, I was mad at myself, frustrated at having made the wrong choice not to get on the bus, and angry that they even have good shops versus bad shops depending on your neighborhood. My inner BJ was screaming, "Girl, just go on back because this place is much further than you realized, and that little dress ain't worth all this. Wear your Kmart dress and call it a day!" I jest, but the battle was real.

Truth is, spiritually, I know what it's like to reach that point of questioning my every move and contemplating the turn back. I was tired, truly worn out from the battles of near defeats and the constant struggle to regain consciousness. Even the little things seemed insurmountable. I'm going to be late, what will people say? Is this blouse too revealing? Did I overstep my male co-leader's authority? Did I serve enough today? At times, I just wanted to close my eyes, let the exhaustion slip away, and give up the fight. But, like the trip to the mall, every decision to go a little further drew me closer to my destination. It was one small decision after another. Remembering, either way, the investment of time and effort has been made. If I give up the fight, the whole journey was pointless. If I keep pushing forward, there is at least a reward at the end. In that very space, the peace that transcends all understanding engulfs you. I know that's probably the most religious thing I can say. It's like talking to your grandmother: "Everything's gonna be all right, baby. Just trust God." But the fact of the matter is, it's true. Grandma was right. It's a calmness that makes no earthly sense. The battle is still raging. The outcome is still unknown. The direction is still unclear. Maybe this is exactly where God wants me to be, in a place of no longer fighting against His will in my life. Lost, but inside the man who holds the compass of the world in the palm of His hand. That place where the drowning victim ceases to fight the rescuer.

At times in my kindergarten class, one of the little ones will come up and tattle in wide-eyed disbelief and amazement that little Tommy used the "S" word, "stupid." The room erupts in a sea of "Oooh, you're in trouble." And at first, my grown-up mind would race to *how does little Tommy even know the "S" word? Do I need to call home?* Well, God's "S" word has the same effect on us. We become wide-eyed, a little panicky, and uncertain of what to do. God's "S" word, however, isn't "stupid," but "surrender," that strange place where what feels like accepting death is embracing life. That intersection where you are forced to choose to breathe or die.

A wise woman shared something prophetic with me one day that radically changed my life. She said, "BJ, your world has exploded around you so many times, but because you are a survivor, you refuse to go down. So, you grab your pieces and force them back together and, almost immediately, begin to rebuild. The only problem with that is like with a jigsaw puzzle, you can force pieces into places they don't belong. They don't fit. So God keeps re-exploding your foundation because He wants you 'not' to grab the pieces, but instead put your hands behind your back, take a deep breath, and let Him put the pieces where they actually should be. You see, the foundation you are building on cannot sustain you for the mission He's calling you to."

That profound statement rocked my world. I knew in my gut that she was right, but I also knew it would be the toughest fight of my life because putting my hands behind my back and not saving myself was a foreign concept. Every fiber in my body pushed back against that. It's like falling off a bridge and not waving your arms to brace for the impact. It's instinctual. Part of me was thinking, lady, you must be crazy, while another part of me knew that in her words was the truth. I began to revisit some of those "life explosions" she had hinted at. Those places I'd conveniently forgotten, tucked away in a place they could never hurt me again. And a pattern started to emerge. With every hit, every sting, every burn, like a little child in protection mode, I would brace myself for the blow and wait to exhale. For decades I had been holding my breath while clutching my sea of lost dreams.

Thirty-five years ago, my young marriage, although riddled with abuse, was all I knew and marriage was precious to me. As it crumbled around me, I fought for dear life to hold on. Leaping from every paper and magazine, all the experts shouted, "Never stay in an abusive situation." Meanwhile, the religious preached, "God hates divorce." An unsuspecting family, not knowing what was going on behind closed doors, said, "Tough it out. All marriages have challenges."

The little girl, afraid to speak, resurfaced. I was paralyzed. Afraid to go, afraid to stay. The fear-stricken child uttered what would become her battle cry for the rest of her life: "God, I can't breathe!" I didn't know what to do. So afraid of disappointing God, I felt I was damned if I did and damned if I didn't. Standing outside the home of a friend hosting a church leaders' meeting that I was supposed to be a part of but had no desire or confidence to go into, I waited. Mind made up: I was done. I couldn't do this anymore. For some reason, I felt pulled to at least say goodbye to my friend before throwing in the towel. Seeing me outside the window, knowing I should be inside, she pulled me in and said to wait until they were done.

I sat there, desperate for the meeting to end so I could run out. True to fashion, they circled to end in prayer, and she reached out to pull me in. Everything inside me pushed back against it. You see, God and I were done. Like a breakup with a boyfriend, I wanted nothing more to do with Him, but appearances, as you know, were everything to me. So reluctantly, I stood, circled, and held hands, prepared to let them do their prayer thing. Then, caught completely off guard, she said, "BJ, will you pray for us?"

My heart pounded. Conversations in my head raced. We stood for what seemed like minutes in silence, and to my surprise, no one said a word. They just waited. Then, barely audible, empty, with no words left to pray, I simply said, "God, help me."

Those three words saved my life. As if the whole room knew that no other words were coming, all simply said, "Amen." My friend turned to me in tears, wrapped herself around me, and said, "I will not let you go."

I recall when finally walking out of my marriage with only a suitcase, my eight-year-old cat, and a 16-inch black and white TV, tears streaming down my face, heart pounding, free, but terrified of the unknown. At that moment, the television celebrity vanished as a broken young woman wandered into what felt like the deepest darkness. Desperately needing a hug, but cringing at the thought of touch, I felt my skin had been ripped from my body. I was raw, shattered by the loss of a dream. I braced myself for the blow and waited to exhale.

Everything frightened me. I fought out of fear. I ran out of fear. I succeeded out of fear. I failed out of fear. It was my constant companion. I recall one of our many unruly pastimes as kids was jumping off the top of the house onto a pile of clothes underneath. I know it's crazy, but to my nine-year-old brain, it was thrilling to do what my brothers did. Until, that is, dad got home. The minute I saw his old, beat-up car coming down the street, I froze! I could either jump down, *which I was terrified to do,* stay standing on top of the house and meet my dad's wrath, *which I was terrified to do,* or get pummeled by my brothers for getting us all in trouble, *which I was terrified to do.* To the yells and screams of "Jump, jump, jump!" I finally jumped down and sprinted inside to hide behind a door. I nearly passed out when my dad opened the door, asking what I was doing on top of the house. There I stood, exposed.

Over the years, I've come to see just how right my siblings were. My fear became the face of my shadow, my personal boogie man. If I wanted to breathe again, I had to, at some point, stand face to face with it. Oddly enough I've played childhood games trying to catch my shadow or hide from my shadow only to find that wherever you go it's still there. Who knew that little game was a precursor to a deeper life lesson? Your shadow, your boogeyman, is always present. You just can't always see it.

Matthew 7:7 says, *"Ask and it will be given to you; seek and you will find; knock and the door will be opened to you. For everyone who asks receives; the one who seeks finds; and to the one who knocks, the door will be opened."*

So, I began to ask God, "If I am not afraid when I don't see my shadow, my boogeyman, why am I so afraid when I do?" Interestingly enough, He led me to Psalms 23, a passage I've read and loved all my life, but now He was leading me to a deeper understanding.

*"Yea though I walk through the valley of the shadow of death, I will fear no evil for Thou art with me."*

His answer: "Because when you see *it*, you don't see *me.*"

I had to sit quietly and meditate on that truth. I know all the scriptures, I've heard the sermons and read the books about keeping my eyes on Jesus. So why does this feel somewhat different? The truth is, I'd tried to apply adult reasoning to a simple childhood principle: any object blocking the light creates a shadow in front of you. If the object is behind the light, the shadow is still there, but you can't see it. Most importantly, the shadow only exists *because of the light*. I paused as I pondered the depth of that statement, then my familiar friend, tears, began running down my face as I realized how profound that little revelation is. God had just revealed the mystery to my freedom. The boogeyman that has so threatened my spiritual life all of these years only has that power when I allow it to stand in front of my light. When our problem(s), large or small, block our view of God, it creates a shadow in front of us so frightening that it cripples us, bringing us to a standstill. And where are shadows most prominent? In the valley. Because valleys are surrounded by mountains or hillsides. In other words, light blockers.

Life is walking through the valley of the shadow of death.

I've heard preachers expound on the seasons of life by contrasting the valleys and the mountaintops. The mountaintop is where we want to dwell. It's the moments we cherish, the moments we hold up as examples of great faith. Shout from the mountaintop! The valley, however, we view with a whole different perspective. It is the place we want to escape or avoid at all cost, but what we fail to understand is that we are most often in the valley. Maybe the terrain changes and in those times, we are more aware of the struggle, but the valley is our day to day. It is the norm, not the exception. So why do I get down on myself when I find myself trudging through the darkest valley as if I've done something wrong and am being punished?

Again, I hear Him say, "Because when you see *it* (the shadow), you don't see *me* (the Light)."

BJ, the valley is the place that provides the necessary moisture for crops and pastures to grow. It's where shepherds intentionally lead their sheep to rest, graze, and regain their strength after the long, hard, weary toll of climbing to the mountaintop.

*"He makes me to lie down in green pastures; He leads me beside the still waters. He restores my soul." Psalm 23:2*

If you are to spiritually rebound, you *must* change your view and embrace the valley.

You see, I have viewed the valley as a place of struggling to survive rather than the place where I learn to survive the struggle. To me, it has been the place where being overwhelmed steals your breath away, slowly claiming your life. But Father, You say it is where I lead you so that your life can be restored. Made whole. Made new again. You are "The Light" in the shadow-filled valley, giving me the life-giving moisture I need to grow.

You created the valley as my protection from the harsh storms and winds, yet I've viewed it as a place of isolation and punishment and disappointment. A self-imposed "land of the misfit toys." The place where those who don't fit get left behind and forgotten. Instead, You are "The Light" guiding me through the shadowy valley, protecting me from storms I can't see.

I get it now. It's surrendering and embracing life, mountaintops, and valleys on God's terms.

Watching a loved one face death reveals secrets that you can't understand until you find yourself in God's waiting room, listening for your own name to be called. Just months ago, I helplessly stood, watching my dad in his final valley of the shadow of death, his life swiftly coming to an end. Just weeks earlier, he stood at the Thanksgiving table, telling the kids, "It's time you take this huge family dinner responsibility off your mother. From this point on, this is all on you. We've put in our time." Did he somehow know that come Christmas, he would no longer be there to protect Mom from our selfishness?

Now, days after that pronouncement, we all stood supporting the mom who had given her whole life to us as she prepared to say goodbye to her life partner of sixty-two years. There was no more human fight, no meds or special treatments, all human efforts had been exhausted. He came to the Passover, that place where God's will is in motion and it carries you into your destiny. You can't stop it or delay it. Your job is to just surrender, to breathe until the master says, "No more." I leaned down and, in his ear, quietly sang his anthem song, "All to Jesus, I Surrender," as this gentle giant ebbed from this world to the next. The pain, hurt, regret, and battle scars endured in the valleys of his life had altered who he had become. With God, nothing is wasted. There had been reasons for enduring every valley, and one of those reasons was me.

*You intended to harm me, but God intended it for good to accomplish what is now being done, the saving of many lives. (Gen. 50:20)*

Every hero of the faith encountered their valleys and ultimately came to this Passover.

When Joseph was a young man, he had a dream that his brothers would bow down to him. They hated him when he told them the dream. He then had another dream showing not only his brothers bowing to him but also his father and mother. His brothers were so angry they wanted to kill him. Instead, they threw him into a pit (valley), sold him as a slave (valley), and he was then falsely accused of raping his master's wife (valley) and thrown in prison (valley). *"It was nearly 14 years between his dream (the mountaintop) and the time he left prison (the valley) to become second in command of Egypt."* Genesis 41: 1-57

Joseph had to tell his heart to beat when I'm sure there were times in the valley he wanted to die.

When David was a teenager, he was anointed as the next king of Israel. It was then that he faced Goliath (mountaintop), but the beloved King David was not loved by everyone. He was banished by Saul (valley), hid in the desert (valley), lived on the run (valley), forced out of the nation (valley), and fought many battles (valley). *"It was nearly 15 years between the time that he was anointed king (mountain top) and actually taking the throne."* 2 Samuel 2: 1-5

David had to tell his heart to beat when I'm sure there were times in the valley he wanted to die.

Moses, the deliverer of the Israelites, was commissioned by God at the burning bush (mountain top). Then the Israelites grumbled in the wilderness (valley), he was blamed by the people (valley), attacked by the Amalekites (valley), overwhelmed and overlooked (valley). *It was forty years between the burning bush commissioning from God (mountain top) and his wandering in the desert (valley).*

Moses had to tell his heart to beat when I'm sure there were times in the valley he wanted to die.

So much living took place between their start and their finish. It is their journey, the mountain tops *and* the valleys, that inspire us. Without their pain, we would know no power. Without their injustices, we would have no tolerance. Without their perseverance, we would have no hope. Though we see it not at the time, someone is observing how we navigate through our valleys as a guiding light through theirs. A beautiful poem by Linda Ellis called 'The Dash' speaks eloquently of the impact of our lives while here on this earth.

As Christians, our dash consists of the mountain tops and the glorious valleys of our lives that shape us into the friends, lovers, co-workers, and agents of light that God intended us to be. How are you living your dash?

Staging a spiritual comeback is walking backward to walk forward. It's remembering why you ventured on this road to begin with, taking a look at how far you've traveled, and how much you've overcome, and being willing to recalibrate if necessary.

If you find you've wasted a lot of time traveling down the wrong road…turn around. Paul, the apostle of God, had to do it.

If you find you're weary and exhausted from the journey…rest. Elijah, the Prophet of God, had to do it.

If you find the road is steep and ever daunting…surrender. Jesus, the Son of God, had to do it.

God is never off the job. It is we, in fear, ignorance, and frustration who abandon the post.

*Be strong and courageous. Do not be afraid or terrified because of them, for the Lord your God goes with you; he will never leave you nor forsake you.*
*(Deut. 31:6)*

In other words...*breathe!*

## NAKED REFLECTION

## Theme Scripture: Rom. 8:28

> *"And we know that in all things God works for the good of those who love him, who have been called according to his purpose."*

**Prayer:** *Father, I stand amazed at how You execute Your plans. How You knit together every intimate detail of salvation before time began. What seems unfair, cruel, or harsh at the time, You bring to completion in bold, beautiful, and glorious ways. You always work it for Your good and Your glory. Help me to trust You today in my hard place. The place I don't understand. Help me believe with all my heart You are working to fulfill Your purpose and my good. In Jesus' name, amen.*

## NAKED STUDY

**Q.** Reflecting over your life's journey with God, identify and share the times you've had to tell your heart to beat again. What spiritual muscle(s) was God developing?

_____

_____

_____

_____

**Q.** List the shadows in your life, the scary places that loom, and in prayer, bring them before God.

_____

_____

_____

_____

_____

**Q.** How have the shadows in your life impacted you?

_____

_____

_____

_____

_____

**Q.** The shadow only exists because of the light. Write down where you see God's presence in the shadow of your valley.

_____

_____

_____

_____

_____

**Q.** Spend time thanking God for the valley He put you through and share it with someone today.

_____

_____

_____

_____

_____

_____

_____

# NOTES

# 8

## SPIRITUAL RESUSCITATION

Honesty, support, and change.

Rushed to the campus hospital, doctors aggressively ran tests, prodded, and probed, trying to assess what was going on. Passed out, bleeding from my mouth, nose, and ears, under constant monitoring and around-the-clock care, what had happened to this young girl that she was found unresponsive on a college campus bathroom floor? No drugs or alcohol in her system, but an erratic heartbeat, and pulse racing. Did she have some undiagnosed disease? The medical team worked frantically to restore normal signs of life. Resuscitation is forceful, violent, and scary, even ugly. As they are cutting, ripping away at clothes, no one cares if your hair is in place or your makeup is smeared. The only thing that matters is getting the person stable. Getting them to a place where you can begin to assess the root cause.

After three long days, baffled, the doctors asked, "Is there anything you can tell us that might help us? Anything we need to know? All your vital stats are back to normal, so we're going to release you, but something had to bring this extreme reaction on."

Shaking my head as discharge papers were being signed, I said, "Nothing I can think of." I walked out the doors...never mentioning that I had been struggling with an eating disorder for years, had been purging a number of times a day, was exercising incessantly, and was growing increasingly weaker with each episode.

Desiring to stop but now unable to control it, it seemed to have taken on a life of its own. An all-consuming, all-encompassing life. The foods I ate were determined by what came up the easiest. The clothes I wore or didn't wear were regulated by their ability to cover up whatever, in my deranged mind, needed shielding from the world. I had mastered the art of carrying around a plate full of food at a gala, moving it around but never really eating anything in public. It was a full-time job covering up the lie. I'd experienced near collapse before, a little lightheadedness, but the bleeding was new and it scared me. Now, with my life literally on the line, I needed to choose, hold on tight to the lie, or finally get real.

Likewise, spiritually I had been unresponsive for a long time hiding behind unhealthy habits. Having a form of godliness, but denying His power. If I was going to be spiritually resuscitated, it had to start with me being gut-level honest with myself and with God. There have been many twists and turns along my spiritual journey where I needed to sit out of the limelight and wrestle with the Almighty. Times of resentment, distrust, and grievances that without heart resolution made it impossible to be who He was calling me to be. But unlike Jacob, stopping everything and wrestling with the angel until he received his blessing, I continued for much too long disconnected from the Father.

Somewhere along the way—maybe it's age, I don't know—I hit the wall. I saw the ridiculousness of my life spinning in circles. I wasn't living, but simply buffering. My busyness, even if done in the name of Jesus, only served as a cushion from getting truthful about my hurts, pains, and disappointments, and I just couldn't do it anymore. Not the ability to do the work, but the heart to do it. Underneath all of my mess, what I desired most was to please God. And when I knew in my soul that I was no longer pleasing Him but was instead grieving the Holy Spirit, I gave up my fight.

I recall praying, "Father, tell me where to go and I'll go. Show me what to do and I'll do it. Speak Lord, your servant is listening."

As He always does, He answered. *"Come to me, all you who are weary and burdened, and I will give you rest. Take my yoke upon you and learn from me, for I am gentle and humble in heart, and you will find rest for your souls. For my yoke is easy and my burden is light." (Matt. 11:28)* I came to realize that I wasn't this horribly sinful, you-probably-shouldn't-even-be-in-ministry person that the negative voices in my head constantly screamed at me, but a strained sheep laboring under a Herculean task because she hadn't learned to do this Jesus' way. *So* figuratively speaking, I crawled into bed, turned the lights off, and pulled the covers over my head. It was time I stopped ministering to others and allowed the great physician to minister to me. I say it that way really for the benefit of my fellow ministers. I never stopped doing the work of the Lord, it is my calling, but I learned to put myself first so that I had a clean vessel to minister out of. Only then did I discover that what once crushed me truly became, as Jesus promised, easy and light.

Singer David Bowie was once quoted as saying, "Aging is an extraordinary process where you become the person you always should have been." After all these years, I guess I'm finally embracing aging and becoming who the Maker created me to be.

It took a few more years before I got honest and sought help with my eating disorder as I moved from college into an industry that secretly supported and sometimes encouraged the lifestyle. Spiritually, however, I didn't have that luxury. If I was going to survive, I needed to surround myself with people who cared more about me than what I brought to the table. A support team that didn't secretly encourage my behavior, but would say no for me when I wouldn't say it for myself. Those who would allow my ugly to pour out and not judge me for it or run away from me because of it. Friends who allowed me to be a person first and minister second. A good friend is not as easy to find as you would think, but well worth the effort it takes to do so. Surprisingly, they don't always come in the packaging you'd expect. At least they didn't for me. My preconceived idea was that leaders befriended other leaders because we ran in the same circles, but I learned we also shared the same struggles and often the same bad habits in dealing or not dealing with them. In doing so, I found myself like with fellow actors stuck in the vicious cycle of an eating disorder, turning a blind eye to what could very possibly claim their life.

Hearing my cry from years earlier, walking down the steps of that church when I silently screamed, "I don't want to be a star here. I need a safe place to fall at the feet of Jesus and be free to be the mess that I am." I believe in that very moment God began assembling my support team and moving us all into position for Operation Rescue BJ. They helped me preach my pain rather than just my victory. Stand in my brokenness and proclaim the glory due to the Savior rather than hide it away as something too shameful to be acknowledged. They emboldened me to let my strength shine through my weakness. *"That is why, for Christ's sake, I delight in weaknesses, in insults, in hardships, in persecutions, in difficulties. For when I am weak, then I am strong." II Cor. 12:10*

As the doctor had spoken decades earlier, all your vital stats are back to normal so we're going to release you, but something had to bring this extreme reaction on. It was time to deal with what landed me here. Now solidly rooted in honesty and surrounded by a strong support team, it was time to face what had to change in my walk. I can't say this loudly enough: resist the urge to fix yourself! I had to resist the urge to soul search and ask myself because, you see, I had already tried and used up all my human solutions. *"Are you so foolish? By beginning by means of the*

*Spirit, are you now trying to finish by means of the flesh?" (Gal. 3:3).* It would have simply landed me back where I started. Instead, *I entrusted myself to him who judges justly* (1 Pet. 2:23).

Desiring nothing less than total restoration, I was led to II Pet. 1:3-11: *3 His divine power has given us everything we need for a godly life through our knowledge of him who called us by his own glory and goodness. 4 Through these he has given us his very great and precious promises, so that through them you may participate in the divine nature, having escaped the corruption in the world caused by evil desires.*

*5 For this very reason, make every effort to add to your faith goodness; and to goodness, knowledge; 6 and to knowledge, self-control; and to self-control, perseverance; and to perseverance, godliness; 7 and to godliness, mutual affection; and to mutual affection, love. 8 For if you possess these qualities in increasing measure, they will keep you from being ineffective and unproductive in your knowledge of our Lord Jesus Christ. 9 But whoever does not have them is nearsighted and blind, forgetting that they have been cleansed from their past sins.*

*10 Therefore, my brothers and sisters, make every effort to confirm your calling and election. For if you do these things, you will never stumble, 11 and you will receive a rich welcome into the eternal kingdom of our Lord and Savior Jesus Christ.*

He was saying, "BJ, this time let's make your calling and election sure." And for the next eight months, I sat at the foot of the cross, combed through with honesty and a truth support team, every element listed in the passage above to see where I was lacking. Starting with faith. What was the condition of my faith? Was it an eroded faith that slipped away underneath me when challenging times came? A faith rooted in fear that paralyzed me in the darkest hours? Faith rooted in failure, weak and limited by my past mess ups being played over and over again in my head? A faith rooted in folly neglected and abandoned, summoned only when I found myself in a jam? Some of you may be thinking, well that's not faith. The teacher in me challenged that. Faith, we know, is being sure of what we hope for and certain of what we do not see. If I'm certain I'm going to fail, I have faith in that. If I'm sure danger is going to overtake me, I have faith in that.

So, you see, it isn't a matter of having faith. We all have it. But the condition of that faith determines if it's worth standing on. To reach a faith rooted in freedom, I first had to get honest, get help, and be willing to make a change.

The young girl who fell in love with Jesus so long ago and for decades wandered in search of Him found Him deep inside of herself. She started at faith, faith the size of a mustard seed, but found He ended at love. The distance between the two is too great a leap—trust me, I tried—so the gap had to be closed by developing spiritual stepping stones that led one to another. Having been taught that faith alone would sustain me, I never knew that in between I needed to be at work building, adding to my God-given faith the unwavering goodness of who He is. Something I would desperately need to fall back on in good times, but especially in bad. True knowledge of Him, because what I think dictates how I feel, which dictates what I do. Self-control to not fall prey to impulses and irrational thoughts, no matter what industry you're in, coming at you every day. Perseverance to stay the course, not run away or bury my head in the sand, and allow the rough waters to form my character. Godliness, the emotional liberation, ascension from what's natural (instinctual, earthbound) to what's supernatural (spiritual, heavenly). Brotherly kindness, that eternal interconnectivity. The reality that we all need somebody, and somebody needs us. We are, like it or not, our brother's keeper. Then finally reaching the open arms of the Father in that peaceful sweet spot called love.

It's taken me decades to finally get here. To REBOUND!

Hello God, it's me...

I'm so glad to finally meet you.

BJ

## NAKED REFLECTION

### Theme Scripture: II Cor. 6:11-13

*"We have spoken freely to you, Corinthians, and opened wide our hearts to you. We are not withholding our affection from you, but you are withholding yours from us. As a fair exchange—I speak as to my children— open wide your hearts also."*

**Prayer:** Father, I recommit myself to You today. I willingly place myself on the table. Take my heart, wounded and closed. Open it wide so that I can receive the love You pour out on me. Help me to be honest with my pain, vulnerable allowing in help, and to change so that I cannot be shaken. Help me to Rebound. In Jesus' name, amen.

## NAKED STUDY

The bleeding woman was determined to go to any length necessary to reach Jesus. For twelve years she searched. For twelve years she faced disappointment. For twelve years she heard no. But all she needed was one yes, and that yes from the mouth of the Savior, Jesus Christ.

**Q.** What are you begging God for that seems impossible to all around you? You'll never rebound if you're not reaching for something higher than yourself.

_____

_____

_____

_____

_____

_____

_____

**Q.** How far are you willing to go for your yes?

_____

_____

_____

_____

_____

_____

**Q.** Do you have a support team, and if so, do they know in detail the battle(s) you're facing? If not, why or why not?

_____

_____

_____

_____

_____

_____

**Q.** If honesty is the key to saving your life spiritually, whats keeping you from getting gut-level honest?

_____

_____

_____

_____

_____

_____

# Epilogue

## PATIENCE AND DETERMINATION

This is the end of the road. The place where I jump off and hope you hold on. Like a mother weaning her baby, you hope that you have done enough, encouraged enough, challenged enough and prayed enough. Ultimately, however, you have to let go.

Watching my then 21-year-old daughter take her first international flight without me, heart pounding out of my chest, but playing the role of the secure, progressive mom, I smiled. She stood with other college students, looking very much like the little girl, taking off without her parents for the first time, also pretending not to be scared and all grown up. The unsure mom inside lingers long, not wanting to leave. Blurting out questions like, do you have enough money? Is there anything else that you need? You have your phone, right? Praying everything goes well, and that everything she has been taught, holds.

That moment in time captures the exact feelings at the end of writing a book. Your work is done, now it's time to let go and hope that it hits the mark.

Whatever your journey is that led you to pick up this book I pray that you will hold on because the reward at the end is so well worth it. I am not deceived, and acknowledge that we live in a hurry and get it done society. One where the very idea of something taking time is distasteful to us. So I'm sorry to say, Rebounding will take time. The very meaning of the word; to bounce back from impact or injury implies work and effort.

Sportswriter, David Murphy once wrote about the late, great basketball legend, Kobe Bryant, "I'm not entirely sold on the fact that Kobe Bryant is a human being". They had witnessed him play through all sorts of game ending injuries and rise from the ashes, but this one, the tearing of his Achilles heel was too much to recover from. Even after undergoing successful surgical repair of the tendon, he now faced months of rigorous rehabilitation. With anticipation high and expectations, low many questioned his ability at 34 to fully recover and continue to be a valuable, dominant force for the Lakers.

Lessons from his arduous and meticulous process, however, would serve us all well. He said in an article, "First, right there on the spot, I tried to feel if the tendon was there or if it was gone." He took time to assess his situation. Then he said something profound, "I was really tired. Tired in the locker room, upset and dejected and thinking about this mountain to overcome. I wasn't sure I could do it. But then your kids walked in and you're like, I gotta set an example. Daddy's going to be fine. I'm going to work hard and go from there." He found his reason to fight. And to everyone's surprise, after 8 months of strategic and focused rebuilding, the Black Mamba was back!

Staging a spiritual comeback is no different, you must assess your situation and find your reason to fight. I found my situation was dire and I was barely holding on. That may or may not be you, but until you do an honest assessment you will never know. Then find your reason to fight. It might be your kids, your health or even your mental health. Stress does strange things to people. Mine was my God, I didn't feel I could live another day apart from him and it was worth the fight to get to him. Whatever your reason, use it to fuel your battle. You'll need it in the times you want to quit.

Lastly, don't be afraid to let pride propel you. We always speak of pride in the negative, but there are instances when it becomes your rocket fuel to the top. The article went on to say, "this is the strongest-willed player since Michael Jordan... If anyone is going to come back from this injury stronger than ever, it'll be the Black Mamba." And come back he did!

Of course the question now was, will Kobe be Kobe again? Will he be the player he once was? Afterall, the superstar was now running around on legs that had carried him for more than 54,000 NBA minutes. There will always be naysayers. Bryant, possibly for one of the few times in his life, was the underdog. But we all know how it ended, Kobe Bryant, a five-time NBA champion, famously scored 60 points in his last NBA game at the age of 37.

Though deeply injured and sidelined, we get to decide our ending.

If you're anything like me your journey will take time, because it is a process. A process of growing as a person, of understanding who God is and who he isn't, understanding not just what's happened, but why it's happened. The lesson behind it and what it says about the maker and what it says about you. Those things are not to be rushed.

So much of what I needed in my future was left scattered on the ground of my past. This journey has taught me to pick up those pieces, brush off the pain of it, embrace the lesson and bring it with me. It's now become the rungs on the ladder to my destiny.

So resist the urge to speed through. Resist the urge to give up. Resist the urge to settle for less. Don't take this journey alone. In the naked reflections I'm asking you to be so honest that it hurts. And the most honest of us are not that honest. This is when you discover who your real friends are. Those who would tell you the truth no matter what. Journey with a friend. Journey with a study group. Journey as a church. As children of God let's return to an intimate relationship with the Father.

My daughter made it on her trip. She spent a month in Israel far away from me and the rest of the family. I sweated. I prayed and I waited. Ultimately, I had to trust that what I had taught had truly been gained and what she did not know, God would protect and carry her the distance. There were bumps in the road and there were also wonderful miracles. Letting go is hard to do, but we'll never see the miracles until we try.

It's time to REBOUND.

# ABOUT THE AUTHOR

**Belinda "BJ" Foster** is a native Texan and has been married for the past 25 years to evangelist Kai Foster. Residing in Southern California while raising a family and serving in the ministry for more than two decades, they now call Reno, Nevada, and the beautiful Northwest their home. She is the proud mother of two wonderful children: a daughter, Mason (24), and a son, Cole (21).

Given the nickname "BJ" at childhood, she was raised in Dallas in a tiny, two-bedroom, one-bath house with six siblings, a loving mother and father, and the occasional stepbrother and sister during most Texas summers. Of course, that's a lot of people in such a small space, but you learn to find your way quickly while daily staking your claim. It was a lower-middle-class struggle and existence with a wide-ranging, neighborhood view of hurting people, people in need.

Once asked as a child, "What do you want to be when you grow up and why?" she responded, "I want to become a singer or an actress because for a few hours on stage I can help people forget their pain." Little did she know that would later become the anthem of her life. BJ became a mother of two, but through many years of shepherding souls and offering solid advice for living, she has certainly become to many a "second mother." Whether helping others find a better way to the Lord or working with underprivileged youth and families providing housing and educational needs in the Reno area, there is never a shortage of love and a giving spirit that flows from her.

After using her many talents and skills for years in network television, on the Broadway stage, and in feature films, BJ heard the loud, deafening cries of many repeating the painful plea that they were just "not enough." She began offering herself and her faith convictions to those who had lost their way and needed to experience something much more. She had overcome her own battles of "Am I good enough?" and then became a deeply empathetic heart of understanding with an outstretched hand of loving acceptance. Since beginning her transforming **More Than Enough Outreach,** BJ has guided women locally and all over the world to see that together with the Creator and one another every chain that binds us can be broken

# Stay connected with me!

**Website:** www.enoughasyouare.com

**Email:** bj.inspiringchangedlives@gmail.com

 http://www.facebook.com/bee.j.foster

 http://www.instagram.com/bee_jayfoster/

This book was published with the support of The Bestsellers Academy.

Do you have a book on the inside of you?

Let us get your story out of your belly and into an international bestselling book!

Phone: 1-868-374-7441

Email: success@thebestsellersacademy.com

Website: TheBestsellersAcademy.com

Printed in Great Britain
by Amazon